1.50

P R A I S E   F O R

From One Single Mother to Another

Sandra Aldrich has written a must-read book for an ever-growing segment of our society, the single mom. Whether by chance or by choice, the single mother needs to have a book such as this as a source of strength, encouragement and just plain practical advice. Job well done, Sandra, and thank you!

Sara R. Dormon and Ruth Graham

Coauthors, *I'm Pregnant . . . Now What?*

Grace is what *From One Single Mother to Another* is all about! Sandra has written eloquently, passionately and persuasively about God's grace in her own life. Her wonderful humor and heart-tugging stories are sure to offer encouragement to every single mom searching for a little hope.

John Fuller

Broadcaster

This is the best book on parenting I have ever read—a great encouragement for single moms who may feel the job of raising children alone can't ever be done properly without a partner. Sandra always finds a way to make her children feel proud of being a famil--

Auth

D1509057

I couldn't put *From One Single Mother to Another* down. I laughed, chuckled to myself and couldn't read the words because of the tears in my eyes. This book is not only for single moms but also for all moms. *From One Single Mother to Another* is a great reference book to keep on the shelf for those "I need help" or "I need encouragement" moments.

Fern Nichols
Founder and President, Moms In Touch International

Sandra Aldrich covers the vast territory of single mothering with humor, sensitivity and tons of practical tips in her book, *From One Single Mother to Another.* A handy resource to be used long after first reading it.

Lois Mowday Rabey
Author, *Daughters Without Dads* and *Women of a Generous Spirit*

As a single mother who raised two children after the death of my husband, I can speak to the treasure that lies in Sandra's new version of *From One Single Mother to Another.* Sandra's wisdom and experience offer single moms freedom from guilt, joy in sorrow, and laughter in the face of fears and tears. She gives practical suggestions and solutions to the nitty-gritty of single parenting. This book is not a pity party; it is an encouraging tool that will empower single moms to face whatever life brings. Woven beautifully through the real-life stories and practical lessons is the love of God and the truth of Scripture. Because I know Sandra, and have seen her live out her faith day to day, I can say that single moms who read her book will know her too.

Bobbie Valentine
Former Executive Producer, Focus on the Family
President, Bobbie Valentine Media Consulting

From One
SINGLE MOTHER
to Another

SANDRA PICKLESIMER
ALDRICH

Regal

From Gospel Light
Ventura, California, U.S.A.

Published by Regal Books
From Gospel Light
Ventura, California, U.S.A.
Printed in the U.S.A.

Regal

Regal Books is a ministry of Gospel Light, a Christian publisher dedicated to serving the local church. We believe God's vision for Gospel Light is to provide church leaders with biblical, user-friendly materials that will help them evangelize, disciple and minister to children, youth and families.

It is our prayer that this Regal book will help you discover biblical truth for your own life and help you meet the needs of others. May God richly bless you.

For a free catalog of resources from Regal Books/Gospel Light, please call your Christian supplier or contact us at 1-800-4-GOSPEL *or* www.regalbooks.com.

All Scripture quotations, unless otherwise indicated, are taken from the *Holy Bible, New International Version®*. Copyright © 1973, 1978, 1984 by International Bible Society. Used by permission of Zondervan Publishing House. All rights reserved.

Other version used is
KJV—King James Version. Authorized King James Version.

Revised edition published January 2005
© 1991 Sandra Picklesimer Aldrich
All rights reserved.

Library of Congress Cataloging-in-Publication Data
Aldrich, Sandra Picklesimer.
    From one single mother to another / Sandra Picklesimer Aldrich.—Rev. ed.
        p. cm.
    ISBN 0-8307-3687-5
    1. Single mothers—United States. 2. Single mothers—United States—Life skills guides.
    3. Single mothers—Religious life. I. Title.
    HQ759.915.A43 2005
    306.85'6—dc22   2004027884

1   2   3   4   5   6   7   8   9   10   /   10   09   08   07   06   05

Rights for publishing this book in other languages are contracted by Gospel Light Worldwide, the international nonprofit ministry of Gospel Light. Gospel Light Worldwide also provides publishing and technical assistance to international publishers dedicated to producing Sunday School and Vacation Bible School curricula and books in the languages of the world. For additional information, visit www.gospellightworldwide.org; write to Gospel Light Worldwide, P.O. Box 3875, Ventura, CA 93006; or send an e-mail to info@gospellightworldwide.org.

Dedication

To my son and daughter, Jay and Holly. Thanks, kiddos, for keeping me from running away to Tahiti—or Kentucky—at the beginning of my singlehood and for giving me lots of reasons to see the joy in each new day.

—Your Grateful Single Mom

Contents

Acknowledgments

During those years of trying to find my footing in my new role as a single mother, I gleaned information from other single mothers as they told me of their trials. So, much of what I share here is from them. And to show my appreciation for the trust they've shown me, I've changed most of their names in these pages to protect their privacy.

But I especially want to thank my sister Thea for sharing insights from her circumstances. Her encouraging calls always came when I needed them most.

Everyone at Gospel Light/Regal Books deserves one of my Kentucky hugs, but several folks went out of their way to encourage this project: Bill Greig III, Kim Bangs, Deena Davis, Marlene Baer, Amber Ong, Bayard Taylor, Amy Friesen and Bill Denzel. God bless you all.

A Letter from One Single Mother to Another

Woe is me for my hurt! my wound is grievous: but I said,
Truly this is a grief, and I must bear it.

JEREMIAH 10:19, *KJV*

Dear Friend:

The book you are holding has been written by this single mom to help and encourage you, another hurting single mom. Perhaps you are new to the reality of "singlehood" and are wondering where to go from here.

The first edition of *From One Single Mother to Another* came out when my two children, Jay and Holly, still lived at home. Today, both are college graduates; they are happily married and gainfully employed. And neither sold drugs, stole cars or turned out to be an ax murderer.

I say all this as an encouragement to those who may be new to single parenting. Too often if we listen to the media, we fear for our children's futures. After all, we hear the tragic stories featuring those raised in one of the 12 million single-parent homes in the United States.

But even though the numbers seem daunting, remember that our children are not statistics. So don't listen to your fears and don't lose hope because of scary reports.

Listen instead to the Lord and draw on your own God-given strength. You *can* walk this path and you can arrive at the finish line—not only as a survivor but also as a victor.

Different Tickets, Same Boat

I confess I never expected to write this book. After all, I'm a Kentucky woman who was raised to take care of a husband and children, have a big garden and make quilts. Parenting children on my own just wasn't part of the deal.

So I've learned far more than I ever wanted to know about being a single mother since that December afternoon when brain cancer defeated my husband, Don, and spun me into single parenthood.

Know then, if you have recently become a single mom and are juggling too many responsibilities, I understand some of what you're dealing with. Much of the spiritual and practical counsel I offer in these pages I've learned the hard way—through lived experience. But don't worry, I won't try to advise you on how to raise perfect youngsters—I never figured out how to do *that*! I simply pray you will find in this book encouragement that comes from the knowledge that you and your children *do* have bright tomorrows.

The divorced women especially have my sympathy. When my husband died, everyone hovered around me—for two weeks—

whispering, "Oh, you poor dear." But when one of my sisters and several of my friends suffered through the process of divorce— one even did so to protect her daughter from sexual abuse—they were treated like lepers. Yes, grief from death is a deep cut, but it's a clean cut. The grief from divorce is deep and jagged.

I also want to encourage those never-married mothers who bravely rejected the option of abortion, who determined instead that with God's help—and, I hope, with that of their local church—they would raise their children themselves. If you are one of these mothers, let me thank you for not aborting your child. God is not finished with any of us yet. And I am convinced He will bring His good out of your wise—and perhaps sacrificial—decision.

And I want to acknowledge all the "married singles"—mothers who are raising their children alone while husbands are in prison, in the military or otherwise absent because of addictions, alcoholism or emotional unavailability.

So, dear ladies, no matter how we came on board, we're all in the same boat. Welcome.

And before we go any further, I need to get one of my pet peeves out of the way: people who constantly refer to single-parent families as "broken homes." Many of us feel that through God's help and a great deal of personal effort our homes have been healed, even if—as in my case—the healing didn't come overnight.

Drawing Strength from Strength

Let me assure you that you *are* stronger than you think you are. In those first days of my own singlehood, I couldn't look ahead to where I am now. While thinking—and worrying—about my single-parenting role, all I could do was look to the examples of strong women in the Bible and in my own family.

I wanted to be like Anna of Luke 2:36—the one who had served in the Temple for most of her adult life. But, unlike Anna, I couldn't withdraw from the world—economics wouldn't let me.

I thought, too, of Molly Pitcher, the woman who carried water to wounded and dying men during the Revolutionary War. Her real name was Molly Ludwig Hays, but as the men called, "Molly! Pitcher!" she gained the nickname that stuck.

During one particularly fierce battle, Molly saw her husband fall beside the cannon he was firing. She ran to his side, not to cradle him in her arms but to take his place and to fire the cannon!

I wanted to be that type of woman! But I learned early that personal strength alone can't conquer all situations.

My great-grandmother Mintie Farley often related stories of the craziness surrounding the Civil War—or, as we call it in Kentucky, the War Between Brothers. She reported that all the men in their little settlement had gone to war, leaving their wives and children alone on the hillside farms.

Although great-grandmother was only a child at the time, she remembered how first one army and then another had stolen everything they could from the farm, including the family's lone milk cow. But late one afternoon horsemen stormed into the yard, demanding the last of the food. Her mother, Stacee Collins, started to argue, but the major merely pointed his pistol at her head and said it would be a shame to have to kill her in front of the children. She gave the soldiers the food.

Over the years—and long after my great-grandmother's death—the story was retold so much and became so real to me that I could have reported the color of the major's hair. As I'd express my indignation, my grandmother Mama Farley would say, "Honey, there are some things in life that all you can do with 'em is bear 'em."

I don't want to *bear* situations. I want them fixed. Now. And in my way. So learning to bear singleness with grace has not been a lesson I've learned overnight; and, human being that I am, I've made plenty of mistakes along the way. I'm much stronger now, but it's taken prayer and personal pep talks to get to this point.

The Single-Parenting Tightrope

Occasionally, my married friends still ask what single parenting is like. My answer: Imagine a tightrope strung across a deep gorge. A single mother gingerly walks across the rope, trying to concentrate on the numerous balls she's juggling. Some have labels: "child care" or "work" or "debt" or "health." Perhaps even "rejection" and "custody battles" are included, but always she's worrying about keeping too many balls in the air at the same time.

On each side of the gorge run folks clamoring for her attention—children, parents, bosses, friends. Then one smooth-talking type gestures for her to step off the rope and join him. At places where the rope dips close to the ground on which he stands, it would be easy for her to drop all those balls and step onto his stony path. But the mother continues on, looking only at the responsibility coming down toward her hand at the moment, knowing if she looks away, she can easily lose her balance.

One of the biblical responsibilities of the Church is to help single mothers keep their balance. James 1:27 calls upon the Church to care for the "orphans and widows." Today, that often translates into providing emotional and financial help for single women and their children—regardless of how they arrived at that status.

I'm thrilled at the growing number of church leaders who have special insight into our needs and who consider single parents as part of their *family* ministry rather than grouping us with the never-married, childless singles. But some churches, it seems, have decided to forgive anything but divorce. I remember the report I received about a woman who was taken by the elbow and "escorted" out of a communion service by an elder the week after her divorce had become final. Ugh!

Single mothers don't need condemnation. We need courage. Speaking for myself, I have always had to battle my own low self-esteem, especially in the beginning when folks said I'd never be able to parent successfully on my own. I've learned that negative thoughts often produce negative actions which, in turn, produce negative results. Psychologists term this phenomenon "the self-fulfilling prophecy."

Remember saying years ago, "Why bother studying for this test? I'm just going to flunk it anyway"? And sure enough, you did flunk it! Well, we can sabotage our future in the same way, if we're not careful.

So instead of yielding to negative thoughts, I set my jaw, looked to the Lord and determined to reach the top of this mountain—just as I hope you are doing. Having survived those early, frightening years, I'm now seeing singlehood as a wonder-ful adventure. If we accept God's help, we do have the hope and assurance that we can be good single mothers.

Yes, go ahead and smile. Better days *are* ahead for you and your children.

So come along, and let me share some of the things I've learned along the way. And may you find encouragement in our shared journey.

Cordially,

Sandra Picklesimer Aldrich
Colorado Springs, Colorado

If I Can Do It, You Can, Too

I can do everything through him who gives me strength.

PHILIPPIANS 4:13

My daughter, Holly, was in third grade when she came home one day in tears. One of the room mothers had handed out printed directions to a special event and said, "Take these home to your families."

Then she'd glanced at Holly and said, "Sorry. I mean 'to your moms.'"

In our Michigan kitchen, I put my arm around my eight-year-old. "Holly, we are still a family," I said. "We're just a family of *three* now."

She leaned against me in relief. That was a turning point for both of us.

That incident, along with others, made me realize that if we were going to survive as a family, we'd have to fight a few emotional battles along the way. And the only way my kiddos could develop their own strength was by watching me.

Sure, We Win Some and We Lose Some, but That's How We Learn

As I share my experiences, let me warn you that I have no pat answers or perfect solutions—and beware anyone who says she has! But I can tell you what worked—and what didn't work—for me and for the other single mothers who shared their experiences with me. And, remember, whatever successes and achievements came our way were rarely the result of any personal innate wisdom. As a rule, they came because of much grace on God's part and much trial and error on ours.

All of us who are raising children alone have too much stress, too many responsibilities and too little time. And no two of us have identical family situations or face identical concerns. So as you read, take note of those ideas and options you feel will benefit you and your family and ignore the rest.

Whatever else I am—a former wife and teacher, a single mom, a writer and an inspirational speaker—my foremost goal in life is to be the woman God created me to be. So, in this chapter, I present some spiritual concerns that are vitally important to all of us, along with some commonplace practical matters we single moms face. Then in each succeeding chapter, I will discuss a particular issue related to single parenting and will offer a smorgasbord of various do's and don'ts as I go along.

Overnight We Become Single Moms, but We Survive Just the Same

I realize the world has changed over the years but one challenge has remained the same: how to raise a family alone. Whether the setting is the mid-1800s Oregon Trail, the 1920s Kentucky coal camps or modern America, the single parent faces hurdle after hurdle. In my own life, I didn't have a clue how I was going to handle all the responsibilities that a single mother must shoulder. I had married young and gone from my father's authority to my husband's. And even though I'd taught in a Detroit suburban school and had handled numerous professional responsibilities, I knew nothing about paying bills, budgeting, balancing a checkbook, doing home maintenance or repairing a car. Those had been my husband's duties.

So without their father, how could I raise my two children to be healthy adults? How could I teach my 10-year-old son to be a man? Even an extended family filled with uncles and cousins did not offer a close-at-hand male relative who could provide the father figure Jay would need.

So I worried and prayed a lot in those first years. I kept us all in church, and I trusted that those couple of hours each week would provide both children with glimpses of what true manhood looked like.

Several years have passed since his dad's death, and Jay's grown up with a mother, a sister and a neutered cat. Yet he has become a masculine young man.

Don't Quit Now

We all have days when things aren't going well, but we single mothers seem to have more than our share. But that's not an excuse for quitting. I remember one long-ago Saturday when my writing wasn't going well. "Ah, Lord, whatever made me think I could write anyway?" seemed to be my most persistent prayer.

Then in the middle of that sluggish morning, Holly arrived home from college and insisted we go horseback riding.

"Might as well," I muttered. "I'm not getting anything else accomplished."

Within the hour, we were at our favorite stable here in the Colorado mountains, but the docile brown horse I usually rode was already on the trail for the entire day. That gentle horse had two speeds—slow and stop—so I was disappointed he wasn't available. There was nothing to do but request the *second* most docile. Soon a large black horse was brought out. We eyed each other for a moment, then I took the reins and led him to the mounting block. There, I placed my left foot in the stirrup and had just started to swing my right leg over the saddle when the horse decided he didn't want me on his back. And he cleverly—and quickly—began to sidestep away from the block. There I was, one foot in the stirrup and the other poised in midair. Even back then I didn't have the agility—or the dainty figure—to shift my weight quickly and throw myself into the saddle. Instead, I was perched in midair for a long moment. The stable owner danced back and forth below me, arms in the air as though to catch me when I fell. There was only one convenient part of my anatomy to push, but he knew me well enough to know he better not try that. So with arms waving, he hopped from foot to foot and yelled, "Don't quit *now*, ma'am! Don't quit now!"

Holly was bent forward in her own saddle, howling with laughter at the scene, so of course I started chuckling and then had an even tougher time hauling myself into position. But finally, with a surge of adrenaline, I shifted my weight and shoved my right foot into the stirrup. The horse gave a defeated snort as I turned his head and followed a still-laughing Holly up the trail.

That ride, even with its tenuous start, proved to be exactly the inspiration I needed to finish the wearisome writing assignment. In addition, that experience has since provided an extra push when I'm tempted to give up. "Don't quit now" is advice that we can't hear too often when it comes to our task of single parenting.

We Can Draw Encouragement from Scripture

I'm originally from Harlan County, Kentucky, and I am proud of my strong mountain heritage. But those who know me best are aware that even as I set my Kentucky jaw, I still occasionally struggle with feelings of inadequacy. In the past, I've even fought a tendency to call myself stupid—especially when I didn't get the hang of something as quickly as I—or a boss—had hoped I would.

In those moments, I played all my mental tapes of every mistake I've ever made. But over the years, I've learned I'm not the only single mother who's trying to fit the ball of good self-esteem into the collection she's already juggling. And I've also learned that every time we beat ourselves up, we're helping the Enemy. And he's one turkey I'm not at all interested in helping anymore than I already have!

That feeling of being woefully inadequate was especially strong early in my singlehood, so I often turned to the Bible for encouragement. Learning that Old Testament women such as Deborah, Ruth and Esther also faced impossible situations and won—with God's help—strengthened me greatly. Soon I was personalizing everything I read in the Scriptures.

One of my favorite accounts of a miracle is in John 11—the raising of Lazarus from the dead. Mary and Martha of Bethany had sent word to Jesus that their brother, Lazarus, was very ill.

Jesus deliberately stalled, until He heard His friend had died. When He finally arrived in Bethany, He went to the grave and told the men standing nearby to roll away the stone (see John 11:38-39).

Then He said in a loud voice, "Lazarus, come out!" (John 11:43).

I'm fascinated that Jesus had to say, "*Lazarus*, come out." I'm convinced that since He is Life, every grave would have given up its dead if He had shouted a mere "Come out!"

When Lazarus emerged from the tomb, he was still bound in the grave clothes. Jesus then said to those standing nearby—surely with their mouths hanging open—"Take off the grave clothes and let him go" (v. 44).

How's that again? The One who raised a man from the dead was asking others to roll away stones and untie grave clothes?

Yes, because He wanted to make a visual point: *Do what you can and leave the outcome with the Lord.* In other words, do what is humanly possible and leave the miraculous stuff to Him.

Even now I'm relieved at the implication here for single mothers: Our Lord will give us the strength to juggle all *our* responsibilities. In faith, we have to do what we can do—and not give up.

It's like the old adage says, "Pray as though everything depends on God, and work as though everything depends on you."

Try Claiming Scripture as Your Own

Isaiah 54:5 is for all single women: "For your Maker is your husband—the LORD Almighty is his name."

Just think. That means we share the same husband, you and I, and I'm not jealous! I drew special comfort from the message of this verse because, before single parenting, I'd never made a major decision by myself and was terrified a wrong choice would jeopardize my children's future. I prayed about everything—large and small. Not only did I get the direction I needed, but I also learned it was okay to argue with the Lord a little bit!

For example, we had just moved into our Colorado home when I noticed the recessed light in the family room ceiling was out. It was time to drag out the tall ladder and change the light-bulb. Perched on the narrow step, I started griping to God. His shoulders are pretty big, and He knows what we're thinking any-way, so He can handle it. Besides, when Jesus said in Matthew 19:14 (*KJV*), "Come unto me," He did *not* add, "But come with a smile on your face" or even "Come without tears." He just said, "Come."

So I told my Husband, God of the Universe, that *husbands* are supposed to change lightbulbs and that I shouldn't have to do this. From there, my complaining quickly escalated to my thinking *I shouldn't have to be doing this single-parenting thing, either.*

When I was griped out, I finally had the good sense to be quiet and listen. In that moment, it was just as though He was saying, "Try turning it the other way."

Try turning it the other way? But I know the lightbulb-changing rule. It's *righty—tighty, lefty—loosey.* But my way wasn't working, so I gave the bulb a halfhearted turn the other way—and it fell right into my hand!

You see, the bulb threads had been stripped, and the pre-vious light changer had forced the bulb into place. God knew the threads were stripped—just as He knows those areas of my life where I am the weakest. I get along in life much better when I listen to Him—and trust those areas of my daily being to Him.

Think Angels and Invoke Our Lord's Protection

In Luke 4:10, God said He would send His angels to protect us. But it wasn't until I was on a church tour that I decided He wasn't teasing.

I'd wandered away from the hotel where our group was stay-ing and had walked for perhaps an hour. Then, as I sat on a low wall to get my bearings so that I could head back to the hotel,

I discovered I was unwelcome: Someone threw stones at me from behind a nearby fence.

Oh, cute, I thought. *Here I am, alone in unfamiliar territory.* I told myself that the stones were being thrown by an obnoxious kid who would take great pleasure in any fear I displayed.

But then I realized that if I'd tried all day, I probably couldn't have come up with anything more thoughtless than walking alone. I took a deep breath.

"Well, Lord, this isn't the brightest thing I've done," I told Him. "But I thank You for the promise that angels are watching over me.

"Now I'd like one special angel to walk beside me. And since angels can take any form they want, I'd like him to be big and ugly—and visible to anyone whose heart is evil."

I imagined my personal angel to be about 6'8" and 290 pounds, with longish brown hair held back with a don't-mess-with-me bandanna. I even nicknamed my angel "Buddy." Then I stood up and, ignoring the stones falling around me, walked confidently all the way back to the hotel with my escort, Buddy, beside me.

When I returned home, I told Jay and Holly about the situation, adding the usual admonishment that we should not purposefully test God by taking foolish risks. Ten-year-old Holly quickly took to the idea that angels watch over us.

So when we moved to New York a couple of years later, she asked, "If Buddy's with us in the hotel, who's gonna watch the truck with our furniture?"

So I created Buddy's twin brother, Buford. I described how he would stand outside the truck, leaning against it as he cleaned his fingernails with a pocketknife. If any kids snooped around the truck, he'd quietly come around the side of the vehicle and say, "I reckon you boys better go someplace else."

Being a Kentuckian, I'm sure *Southern* angels watched over us during that move. The theology here may be shaky, but

Buddy and Buford helped my frightened young daughter—and her mother—to sleep well just the same.

How about you? What have you done during those times when you and your family have needed extra protection? Buddy and Buford have plenty of celestial cousins, so invite them along.

When We Forgo Worry, We See God's Answer

Philippians 4:19 is a verse I claimed early as a single mother: "But my God shall supply all your need according to his riches in glory by Christ Jesus" (*KJV*).

Many times I tested that promise and occasionally challenged Him with "even *this* need, God?"

Gradually, I learned He hadn't overlooked anything. As I learned to pray about every challenge and decision, He answered—though not always as I had hoped.

Sometimes He used friends to show me how to change the oil in the car or to balance the checkbook. Sometimes He encouraged me through a glorious sunset and with the constant thought that He hadn't left me alone.

But most of all He helped me grow; and, as I did, I learned much about myself and even more about my heavenly Father.

Maintain Family Routines

Structure breaks through the daily chaos and often gets us over the rough spots. So having a set time for meals, homework and chores adds needed organization and peace to our schedules. And if we single parents need anything in our routine, it's peace. Regular Scripture reading helps provide that.

It was our habit to read the Bible after weekday dinners and to keep track of our prayer requests in a notebook. Guests, including any of Jay's and Holly's friends who happened to be over for dinner, were invited to join us.

One evening Holly's friend, Jessica, and Jay's German friend, Till, were with us. As we finished our meat loaf, Jay read several of our favorite psalms.

I then explained that it was our custom to take turns praying and that Till was welcome to join us.

He nervously replied, "But I've never prayed in English!"

"Then pray in German," I said. "You're talking to God, not to us. But you don't have to pray aloud if you don't want to. You do whatever makes you feel comfortable."

So Jay opened the prayer time, followed by Jessica and Holly. I was all set to close the prayers when Till hesitantly began to pray. In his first timid words, I caught the word "Deutsch" and knew he was telling the Lord I'd said he should pray in German.

Gradually, his timidity slipped away, and he began earnestly to talk to God. Even though I couldn't understand the words, I understood the emotion—and felt the thankfulness welling up within his prayer.

We would have missed a special blessing that evening if we had set aside our family routine because of guests.

We Must Be Realistic in Our Expectations of Others

Don't Expect Others to Do Everything for You

I remember one young mother who demanded that the men of the church answer her every call for help. If her car tires needed air or if her house windows were dirty, she called on the churchmen to assist her. When they balked—after all, most of them didn't do windows for their *own* wives!—she complained to the pastor, saying the church was supposed to take care of its single women.

That's true, but only to a point. The instructions in James 1:27 direct the Church to provide for their shelter and food, but not for taking over work they can—and should—do for themselves.

Don't Expect Others to Take On Your Hurt

Even though it's been several years since her divorce, Jan still holds a grudge against a woman in her church who didn't respond in the way Jan felt she should have.

In great detail, Jan describes the Wednesday night service when her husband handed her the car keys, said, "Who are we trying to kid?" and walked out.

In that moment, she knew their troubled marriage was over. Numb, she sat through the rest of the service, wanting to give him enough time to walk the few blocks home and to pack his suitcase.

After the service, the woman sitting behind her asked if everything was all right. With tears running down her cheeks, Jan blurted out that she was facing a divorce.

"Then the woman patted my arm, said God would be with me and went home to *her* husband!" Jan says.

Sure, it would have been wonderful if the woman had wrapped her in a hug and said, "Oh, Honey!" but she didn't.

If we're going to think *It's not fair,* and be hurt every time someone fails to provide what we think we need, we're going to get hurt a lot. Other people have their own problems, too, and they can't take on ours any more than we can take on theirs.

Welcome help from others when it comes, but don't demand it. By looking at our situation realistically, we can get through it with less trauma.

Don't Expect Others to Appreciate What You Do

Being a single mom is hard work. Naturally, we'd love to have a pat on the shoulder occasionally, but looking for praise takes energy that would be better used in tending to the duties at hand. Remember, the ancient Greeks didn't award the prize to the winner who crossed the finish line first, but to the one who finished first *with his torch still burning!*

Besides, other folks don't always realize just how much we're doing, anyway. I learned that a while back when a relative and I drove to Kentucky to bring my grandparents, Papa and Mama Farley, and my Aunt Adah back to Michigan.

An eight-hour drive was ahead of us, so my grandmother had an enormous lunch perched next to her on the front seat. On top of the picnic hamper she balanced a bunch of bananas, then settled her cane comfortably against her thigh, ready to begin the trip.

Road construction on the main thoroughfare and numerous detours forced us to wind around the southern hills on dangerously curving stretches of asphalt. Topping one more hill, we discovered a rock slide had covered the road.

The relative who had been driving put the car in park and then got out of the car in order to survey the situation. In the next moment the car stalled and began to roll backward.

I was in the backseat wedged between Aunt Adah and Papa, but it was up to me to reach the brake. In an instant, I threw myself over the seat, knocking the lunch to the floor as I scrambled to stomp on the brakes.

When I finally got the car stopped, it was already several feet beyond the asphalt. And beyond that was a 500-foot drop into the ravine below.

With the car safely braked again, I released my breath and tried to push my heart out of my throat and back down into its proper position. Finally, I looked at Mama Farley. Surely she had some praise for the quick action on my part that had saved the four of us from severe injury—if not death.

But she merely glanced at me as she picked up the scattered lunch. Then she muttered, "You smashed the bananas."

So much for my need for appreciation.

Don't Expect Others to Be There for You Always
Even as I was trying to learn how to juggle all my new responsibilities alone, my dear friends Dick and Rose completed plans to move to California. On the Sunday evening before they left, we said good-bye in my kitchen.

I tried to be brave, but my tears were threatening as I hugged Rose. Then as I turned toward Dick, he gave me such a sorrowful look that I absolutely lost it. All I could do was sob against his shoulder.

My rare display of public emotion created an awkward moment for all of us, but I couldn't stop. Two of my dearest friends were leaving for the end of the world, and I was sure I'd never see them again.

When I finally got myself together, we were all so embarrassed that I determined inwardly I'd never let such a scene occur again, no matter how much I cared about the ones who were leaving. Ironically, several years later, business often took me to Southern California, and I stayed with Rose and Dick whenever I could. I didn't lose them forever, after all.

Even though I had felt at the time that my little raft had just been set adrift, that parting forced me to stop depending on my friends and start searching for my own strength—and that of the Lord. Over time, I found it, too.

Here's What We Must Avoid for Our Emotional Health

Avoid Jealousy and Envy
Jealousy wastes precious energy, but it took me a while to learn that important lesson.

At a business meeting, a man mentioned his wife had hosted a luncheon for several of the ladies from their church. The table was set with crystal and china while the stereo played relaxing music. Each woman had rushed into the house but had been quickly soothed and put at ease by the setting in which they found themselves.

"She created a haven for them," he said casually.

I couldn't comment since I was so envious. Sure, she could provide a haven; she was a stay-at-home wife, who had the luxury of concentrating on her main job—that of taking care of a husband and children.

Her days were her own. She could attend Bible study groups, shop at her convenience, bathe in the afternoon and look nice for her husband—who paid the bills, talked to her and helped her discipline their children. She did not have to juggle those duties and tensions all by herself.

My envy kept me from concentrating, and I confess I can't tell you one other thing that was said during the meeting.

Now when such situations occur, I remind myself that I had my turn at those activities and that I have chosen this lifestyle. True, I didn't choose to be single, but I did choose to raise my children alone, and I did choose to change careers in midlife, after having taught high schoolers for 15 years.

Taking a get-tough attitude with myself helps put things in proper perspective.

Avoid Hurtful Fantasizing

Even though I've come a long way, I still have moments of feeling very much alone. Our first Christmas in Colorado, Jay, Holly and I attended an energetic musical with a thin plot involving a family that gathered in the mountains for Christmas, singing joyful songs and expressing their love for each other.

The show was usually given as part of a dinner package, so even our matinee audience was seated at large round tables. In the final moments before the curtain went up, waitresses hurried between the tables, delivering soft drinks.

When the show started, I was delighted by the high energy of the performers who sang and danced as though they were having a wonderful time. Then, during one particularly tender holiday song, I started to cry, feeling very much alone—even though Jay and Holly were sitting on either side of me.

Just then the man across the table pulled his arm back toward his wife. My tears increased as I realized he was going to put his arm around her and give her shoulders a little squeeze.

How fortunate his wife is, and how wonderful of him to do that. My thoughts were moving faster than the man's arm.

At last, with his arm all the way back, he reached for his soft drink—instead of his wife!

I laughed aloud as another of life's realities brought me back to Earth and shattered one more of my fantasies.

You Help Yourself and Your Family When You Help Others

Since I tend to compare myself with others, the trick for me is to get those comparisons going in the right direction. But I've learned that by reaching out to others, we three could better appreciate what we had left instead of lamenting what we had lost.

That first Thanksgiving after being thrust into single parenting, I decided I wasn't going to cook for the usual mob of relatives. And I wasn't going to accept any of the invitations we received. I knew myself well enough to know that being with two-parent families would only intensify my feelings of loss.

So I called the local Salvation Army to ask if we could help serve dinner. Providing even a small service to others helped me far more than I had expected. And afterward, the three of us went away with a special feeling of peace.

The day had its humorous moments, too. I'd told Jay and Holly to dress warmly that morning, since the dinner would be served in the gymnasium of a little church. I also told them not to wear their nicest clothes since I didn't want us to look as though we were condescendingly "doing our good deed for the year." They apparently followed my instructions too well.

After we had served everyone else, we sat down to eat. Just as we lifted our heads from prayer, a photographer from the local paper stepped through the doorway. He surveyed the room, spotted my blond youngsters, smiled and came over.

"I'm from the local paper, and we're doing a story on families having dinner at the Salvation Army," he said. "May I take your picture? This will be a great shot—you and your kids."

I panicked. "Oh, no! We're volunteers. We've been serving dinner to the others."

He smiled gently. "It's okay. Everybody needs a little help now and then."

"But we're volunteers," I insisted. "We came to help."

An older gentleman at the next table had been watching the scenario with interest.

"You can take *my* picture," he said. "I won't make as pretty a one as the youngins, but I'll smile fer you."

The photographer shrugged and snapped one shot of the man before moving to the other side of the room. I decided that the following year I'd let the kids wear their nicest sweaters.

But I also had to face something deep within my being that I hadn't known was there—pride that we were helping instead of being helped. Even years later, I ponder my reaction. Still, the reporter was right when he said, "Everybody needs a little help now and then." So don't let pride keep you from getting any help your family may need.

Being Willing to Make Changes Opens Us to a Newness of Life

Try New Approaches and Be Pleasantly Surprised

Most single moms at least occasionally hear, "Daddy didn't do it that way," whether we're frying pancakes or cleaning out the garage.

When Melanie's children said such things to her, she used to remind them, "Well, Daddy's not here!" But she soon realized such a retort only deepened the gloom. Finally she forced herself to ask them to show her "how Daddy would do this."

To her delight, Jimmy, her 10-year-old son, remembered how to pour the gasoline into the lawn mower tank without making a mess. Soon she was asking Jimmy how *he* would tackle a task.

Take an Occasional Risk and Grab *This* Moment

We can become so worried about the future—paying bills, making friends, finding a new home— that we miss the joy of *this* moment. This was an especially tough area for me to deal with because I'd always had my security blankets—friends, family, familiar environment—wrapped tightly around me.

But once I forced myself to take little risks, even changing my basic wardrobe color from the pinks my husband bought for me to the deep purples I'd always loved, I discovered I had a heart for adventure. That realization quickly translated into having fun with my young children, including garbage-bag tobogganing near their grandparents' home. I even began keeping a box of oversized bags in the trunk for just such impromptu romps.

Even a walk in the woods became an adventure. And looking back now, we recognize that our favorite memories from those early years of adjustment are in the unplanned events—the trips to the cider mills or free art fairs—not the trips we overplanned for weeks.

Look for the Silver Lining and Enjoy New Experiences

When I was married, Sunday afternoons revolved around football. If I wanted to invite friends for dinner, they had to like football. If I suggested we visit relatives, we had to leave either well before or immediately after the game.

Now these many years later, I confess that while I still miss my husband, I don't miss football one bit.

As I reclaimed those fall and winter Sunday afternoons, I started looking for things Jay, Holly and I could do together. Free museums, plays and symphonies quickly filled the time once belonging to football.

Those activities were some of our choices for a Sunday afternoon; they may not be yours. Maybe visiting with friends and relatives is more to your liking, or taking in a matinee or going to the zoo or whatever. Find new ways to indulge and enjoy!

Analyze and Adjust and Celebrate in New Ways

Altering the way we've celebrated holidays in the past is often the smartest way to handle the challenge of those first holidays that we face on our own.

Just after we moved to Colorado Springs, I had lunch with my realtor, a new friend who was wading through an unwanted divorce. As she sipped her diet cola, she said, "I remember a guy in our office who said nobody invited him to their Christmas parties after his divorce. The holiday is still four months away, and already I'm wondering what I'm going to do."

I shrugged. "That's easy. You and your kiddos are coming to my place for Christmas dinner."

She shook her head. "I can't do that. There'll be five of us."

I insisted I was cooking and if she didn't come for dinner, she'd have to come for leftovers.

Finally she accepted, but only after she insisted we go to her place for Thanksgiving. Suddenly her eyes sparkled at the thought of filling her home again.

Within a few weeks, her guest list consisted of an interesting group of single parents and their children she teasingly called the Lost and Found Gang. We all hit it off so well that I invited *all* of them to my home for a potluck Christmas dinner.

For a long time, the Lost and Found Gang was the core of my social circle. And all because another single mother and I had been willing to analyze our situations and adjust to a new way of doing things.

Let Down Your Hair and Be a Kid Again, Too

Years ago, a preteen Jay and Holly constantly argued over a small blue pillow in the family room. Then I saw teddy bears in a sale bin—soft and fluffy—with tummies just the size of that old blue pillow. I picked out a brown one for Jay and a white one for Holly.

Then as I turned away with my carefully chosen selections, another white bear—this one with a floppy arm—caught my eye. He was imperfect; no one would buy him. Suddenly, with a surge of kinship, I bought him and named him Ralph.

Many nights, after my children had gone to bed, I sat on the sofa, watched the embers in the fireplace and hugged my broken bear. Anyone who's met me in the last few years can't imagine that scene, but maybe I'm stronger now because I allowed myself those evenings of hugging a fluffy bear.

Dare to Do Something Different

Sometimes we have to force ourselves out of our ruts. When things start to close in on Darlene, she takes her children for a walk outside or, in bad weather, in the mall. Their assignment is to see how many different sounds they can identify. The idea is to do something different—and something fun.

Are you one of those who has to have things "just so"? I used to be. But when the New York editorial job offer came, and we moved into a small condo, the cost of living was so high on the East Coast that I couldn't afford wallpaper. So we slapped paint on the walls and moved in.

Within a couple of days of unpacking our boxes, I had hung—with dozens of straight pins—several Amish and Southern quilts to brighten up the rooms. Then on the awkward wall next to the stairs, I hung the scatter rugs my grandmother had braided years ago. Only a few of them were unused; most were ones I had wiped my feet on at her backdoor years ago, never dreaming they'd someday move with me to that great end of the world—New York.

When everything was in place, I stood back to admire the splashes of color against the off-white paint. It was magnificent! What I had originally meant as a temporary measure quickly became my personal decorating signature. Those quilts later adorned my Colorado office and home as well. Often my visitors admire the fabric and then say, "These quilts are so *you.*" And truly they are.

Too Often We Wait to Take Care of Our Health

This is one of those do-as-I-say-and-not-as-I-do sections. I've always been ready to take care of other people, but I'm still learning how to take care of myself.

My weight crept up—and sometimes rushed in—and in the list of priorities, my own health was always at the bottom. It was, that is, until the day I found myself in an emergency room.

At the time, I was working as the associate editor for a Christian magazine in New York and putting in long hours. We desperately needed a secretary to handle the volume of daily mail. My boss had asked the powers-that-be to get us some help, but the response came down that I was handling the situation just fine.

So September 28 had to happen, sooner or later.

That day, we had our usual intense work schedule: Everything was going wrong and deadlines were missed. Then two readers called—they needed to talk to someone about decisions they were facing in their own lives. Because of my grief counseling background, I wound up handling those calls.

Then just about 4:00 P.M., the overnight courier called to say that they'd lost the artwork for the next issue. I numbly heard only that they would continue to check the warehouse.

Next the accounting department needed me. I got halfway up the stairs when my heart threatened to pound right out of my rapidly tightening chest. All of the invisible balls I'd been juggling suddenly clattered as they fell at my feet. I couldn't breathe. I gingerly sat down on the step, convinced I was having an early heart attack.

After several minutes of sitting on the staircase—and praying—I noticed that my heart pounding had grown less intense. So I went into the accounting office.

"Are you all right?" was my friend's quick question.

I nodded. "I'm just tired. It's been a long day."

Quitting time finally arrived, and I called Holly to let her know that I'd be late coming home. Then I drove myself—not a bright idea, by the way—directly to the local hospital.

The examining doctor quickly attached me to an EKG (electrocardiogram). Believe me, something about having wires attached to your chest and being hooked up to machines that beep every few moments puts life into its proper prospective.

My blood pressure was so dangerously high that the doctor was suddenly more concerned about my having a stroke than he was about my having a heart attack. He gave me bitter medicine to hold under my tongue, while I kept thinking about Jay and Holly.

After two hours of running tests, deciding I wasn't having a heart attack after all and bringing my blood pressure down to the high end of the normal range, the doctor gave me the name of two heart specialists for follow-up examinations.

Then he said, "Tell me about your life."

I gave him a wry smile. "Not much to tell. I'm a single mom, raising two teens alone and putting in 12- to 16-hour days on the job."

He nodded. "Want me to admit you for a few days just so you can catch your breath?"

I shook my head. "Nah. I'll sleep better in my own bed," I said. "But I promise to stay home from work tomorrow and see the specialist as soon as he can take me."

He let me go then. And the moment I walked out the hospital door, I mentally left New York, knowing it was just a matter of time before I would take back control of my life. But even the move to a new job and a new state didn't immediately solve my problem. Know what I've learned? Heaven is not here—it is not any place on this earth. So, wherever you are, take care of yourself—just as well as you take care of your children.

Letting Ourselves Laugh Again Is Good Medicine

Giving ourselves permission to laugh again is tough, especially for those of us who were brought up to take care of others and for whom life was serious stuff.

Proverbs 17:22 tells us, "A cheerful heart is good medicine, but a crushed spirit dries up the bones." But even though I knew this truth, it seemed like *forever* before I could allow myself to laugh again.

But laughter did return. And I remember when it happened. A relative was giving an account of one of his zany experiences. I've long forgotten the story he told, but I recall the corners of my mouth turning up as I listened. In that moment, I made a conscious decision to give in to a rib-splitting laugh. And it felt good.

Laughter is not only necessary for bonding with friends but also for good health. Thanks to modern science we know that endorphins—a form of the body's own medicine—are released from the brain when we laugh.

Not only does laughter relieve daily tension, but it also creates marvelous memories—for us as well as for our youngsters. One of my elderly friends says she never heard her grandmother laugh and seldom saw her smile—and then only at other adults. She'd told me that before Jay and Holly turned five, so I asked myself, *If I died now, what would they remember about me?* I didn't like what seemed the obvious answer: "Don't make a mess!"

I decided right then to look for ways to be more fun to be with. The obvious starting point for change was my attitude, so I reminded myself Jay and Holly were still children and not miniature adults. So not only was it necessary for them to clown around and be silly, but it was also okay for me to enjoy their silliness and laugh with them.

Laura's children were ages three and four when their dad took off. Laughing was the last thing Laura wanted to do, but she also knew she couldn't sit in a darkened house and expect the children to be quiet, too. One evening, in desperation, she draped a blanket over a card table and suggested the children play "Indian."

Within a few minutes, the four-year-old peeked out from under the table and gestured for Laura to join them. She opened her mouth to say "No, you just play." But, instead, she said, "Sure!" and thoroughly enjoyed being silly and laughing with her kids. They had let themselves go, and the cheeriness of their time together was indeed "good medicine" for all of them.

What about you? Isn't it time you found ways to lighten your load?

Once More with Feeling

- Draw encouragement and strength from Scripture. Many women in the Bible also faced impossible situations, but they came through victoriously.
- Don't quit. Give that extra push.
- Claim Isaiah 54:5. The reminder that God Himself is our husband helps lighten our load.
- Invoke the Lord's protection and that of His angels.
- Pray—a lot! The Lord helps us, but we have to ask.
- Maintain family routines. Structure often gets us over the rough spots.
- Be realistic in your expectations of others. No one but the Lord can be all we need.
- Know what to avoid. Harboring envy, jealousy, fantasies and the like can only add to our hurt. Longing for what we don't have can cause us to lose the joy of what we do have.
- Try helping others. In doing so, we find peace for ourselves.
- Be willing to make changes. Try new approaches, take occasional risks, dare to do something different and celebrate in new ways. And look for the silver lining—singlehood has its happy moments, too.
- Take care of your health. We're so busy juggling duties and taking care of children we often forget to be good to ourselves, too.
- And let yourself laugh again. "A cheerful heart is good medicine."

CHAPTER TWO

So How Do We Handle Loneliness?

But just as he who called you is holy, so be holy in all you do;
for it is written: "Be holy, because I am holy."

1 PETER 1:15-16

As I entered my second year of singlehood, well-meaning friends asked me when I'd get married again. I laughingly answered I wouldn't even think about that until somebody showed up with a dozen roses. Then I changed the subject.

That evening I mentally replayed the conversation—knowing I often veil the truth with my humor—and asked myself a tough question: *Would I really be attracted to the first guy who handed me roses?*

As I admitted he would at least get my attention, I made an important decision: I would plant my own garden.

The next morning I was at our local gardening shop loading my car trunk with rose bushes and bags of peat moss. For the next several months, I pruned and sprayed—and kept fresh roses throughout the house, quietly marveling at the self-satisfaction I gained from the bright, fragrant blooms.

Slowly I began to "plant my own garden" in other areas of my life as well, even taking steps toward a new career in editing and public speaking. If I had waited for someone else to bring me roses—and "rescue" me from my single state—I would have missed the incredible path my life has taken the past several years.

Hear me: This is not intended to be a soapbox speech for forever singleness. Rather, it's my attempt to encourage you to seek the Lord's direction rather than giving in to a desperate desire to be rescued. If you want to remarry and be part of a new family, go for it. But let the Lord heal you first—please don't wait for someone to show up with life's "roses."

To Remarry or Not to Remarry Is an Individual Decision

Admittedly, I made a tough choice when I decided to put all thoughts of remarriage on hold for 10 years. And although it is not the choice every single mother will make, I know it was the right one for me.

Why 10 years? Well, the women in my family have a history of longevity, so I've often kidded that I plan to live to be 102— and then die of smoke inhalation when my cake, with all the flaming candles, is brought in. And since I believe in the Old Testament concept of the tithe, I decided to tithe my very life. Thus, I chose 10 years to learn more about the Lord and more about myself. After all, I had been Mitch's daughter, Don's wife, Jay and Holly's mother; I wanted to find Sandra Aldrich. And I did. Oh, she's feisty and has a tendency to "shoot from the lip" too much, but she's funny and strong and occasionally even wise. And I never would have found her if I'd thrown myself into another relationship in those early days of single parenting.

I genuinely believe my life would never have turned out the way that it did if I had settled for what my extended family and even society expected, instead of what God wanted to give me. And I believe God wanted to give me more of Himself, not another husband.

I was also convinced the Lord was preparing me for another career, and I felt sure a second husband would just talk me into going back to the high school classroom.

Besides, I'd seen too many problems in second marriages. The divorce rate nationwide is 50 percent for first marriages and 70-80 percent for second marriages. I didn't want to be one of those statistics. So, recognizing that the mortality rate of second marriages is even higher than that of first marriages, I determined to save myself from even risking such a mess.

I was also afraid another husband might be mean to Jay and Holly, and that was something none of us needed. The old adage that "love is better the second time around" may or may not be true. But it's definitely more difficult, particularly for blended families.

Yet, having said all that, wasn't I really hiding from life—as a friend accused me of doing? No, I've searched my heart, and I can honestly say I was not. Rather, I was drawing on the Lord's strength to rebuild my life. And He has continued to do exactly that.

But Your Relatives and Friends Will Still Get In on the Act

Women in my Southern culture are expected to remarry, so I often tried to reason with aunts or cousins who made comments at every family gathering. To keep from saying what I was actually thinking—*That's none of your business!*—I'd often quote

Proverbs 15:1 to myself: "A gentle answer turns away wrath, but a harsh word stirs up anger."

My friend Rose finally helped me break out of that anger trap when she said, "You're giving everyone too much credit when you think they *really* care about your decisions. They don't; they're too involved in their own problems."

I laughed in relief, decided she was right and promptly stopped worrying about everyone's comments about remarriage. Amazingly, as I stopped arguing with the relatives and avoided the topic of remarriage, everyone gradually found more interesting things to talk about.

A friend even said she admired the fact I was *taking charge* of my life rather than merely *reacting* to everything. Then she leaned toward me. "But don't put God and His future for you in a little box."

I thought about that for several days and then prayed, "Lord, You know I want only what You want. But if I can have my druthers, I'd druther remain single. All I need are friends who will smile when I come into a room."

Now that I'm long past the 10-year goal, do I regret my decision? Not for a minute.

Don't Get Burned When Old Flames Rekindle

I was glad I had worked through those various issues the first year of my singlehood because one autumn morning I awakened with the thought *Set yourself apart. Be ye holy.* The idea was so compelling that I immediately started praying for strength to face whatever temptation was coming my way. Deep in my gut, I knew my vow was about to be challenged.

I didn't have to wait long. A couple of weeks later, an old boyfriend—I'll call him Will—came back into my life. He had contacted me shortly after my husband died, but I'd ignored his note. Now he had written again, signing off with the simple "Friends do not forget."

I didn't answer that note either, but I was consumed by it for weeks. I was finding single parenting much more difficult than I'd ever imagined. And I had not yet learned to be comfortable with the silence that pervaded the house once Jay and Holly had gone to bed. More than once I paced the house after they were asleep, thankful Will and I had never been intimate to further complicate my emotions and glad he was several states away.

And now Will was saying softly into the phone, "Let me back into your life."

I stammered, "But I'm not the same person you knew years ago. Besides, I've gained weight."

He chuckled. "You've gained a *lot* of weight. But that's never mattered to me. I've always thought you were terrific."

My thoughts were in a jumble. *A man was saying that the extra pounds didn't matter? And how did he know what I looked like* now? We hadn't talked since the Sunday afternoon 18 years earlier when he'd shaken hands with the one who would later be my husband and told him to be good to me.

Adding to my emotional upheaval was Will's account of the divorce from his alcoholic wife and his admission that he, too, had struggled with a drinking problem in the early years of his marriage. And, to hear him tell it, I had been the cause of all that. "I hit the bottle pretty bad after we broke up," he said into the phone.

We had broken up? And all along, I'd been thinking *he* had broken up with *me*. Obviously, we had been two naïve kids who needed to talk things through, but no one had been there to help us communicate.

Now that I'm on this side of the trauma, I'm shaking my head at all I put myself through back then. Those years were rough since I was experiencing conflicting emotions over the way Will's life had turned out and over the false guilt I felt because of his decision to deal with disappointment through alcohol.

I knew I couldn't go back and undo Will's past pain, and I certainly didn't want Jay and Holly dealing with trauma that had been on the scene long before they were born. So there was nothing to do but lean even more on the Lord and trust Him to bring His good out of my turmoil. And part of His good, I felt, would be in His ultimately using my experience to encourage another confused single mother also struggling with the decision of whether she should reconstruct her life with an old boyfriend.

During that difficult period, I bought a wall hanging on which I embroidered: "Lord, I have a problem—it's me. Child, I have an answer—it's Me."

Grammatically, the expression might not have been right, but theologically, it was perfect for me. In bright green and orange, I embroidered flowers around the brown words and breathed a prayer with every stitch.

In addition to praying, I threw myself into studying God's Word. I joined a Community Bible Study, even enjoying buying the complete works of Josephus, *Strong's Exhaustive Concordance of the Bible* and the *New International Version* of the Bible.

Then in further surrender, I wrote these words in the front of my new Bible:

Lord, these new textbooks and Bible, which have just arrived, thrill me! How thankful I am to be able to study *Your* Word. I meant it, too, when I hugged this Bible to myself and asked You to so fill me with Yourself that everything else is burned away. I want to do only what You want.

When I wrote those words, I was trusting Him to burn away more than just my obsession with Will. After all, once we ask something of the Lord, He doesn't leave it undone. But neither does He do just what we expect Him to do.

The burning away of people, of love of things, of need for familiar surroundings and of total control over my environment didn't come overnight. After all, those attachments had taken me years to develop. But He was working in me, creating a new woman.

Meanwhile, the Lord was also putting things in gear on the East Coast, preparing the way for my eventual move out there. Out of my pain over the way Will's marriage had been destroyed by alcohol, I had begun working with Jim Broome, cofounder of the Detroit-based Alcoholics for Christ. I'd written an article, "What Makes Alcoholics Stop," that summarized many of the principles Jim taught.

Those 2,000 words prompted a New York-based Christian magazine to offer me an editorial position. I quickly accepted—and started a new career that would not have been possible if I'd settled for less than what the Lord had planned.

So, remember, if you're facing temptation, keep talking to the Lord about everything, hang in there and "Be ye holy" (1 Pet. 1:16, *KJV*).

When Ephesians 3:20 tells us that "[Christ Jesus] is able to do immeasurably more than all we ask or imagine, according to his power that is at work within us," it's true!

Maybe you won't be asked to accept a midlife career change and move 800 miles away. But the Lord enjoys giving His children gifts, so who knows what adventures are just ahead for you?

For Some Single Moms Remarriage Is an Option

Make Haste Slowly; Loneliness Can Be a Trap

I'm amazed at the number of women who try to salve their loneliness by rushing into—and staying in—sad, unhealthy relationships. What an awful trap! And the entire time, they keep telling themselves things will get better. Yet they never do.

I learned the illogic of that kind of thinking years ago when I tried to take a shortcut home one beautiful autumn morning. On my day off, I had driven Jay and Holly to school. Because it was such a nice day, I decided to leave the car in the lot and walk the three miles back home. All I had to do was stroll down the school driveway to Joy Road, turn right onto Lilly and head home.

But I looked across the grassy field to my right. *Hmm. If I walk across it, I'll get onto Lilly Road that much more quickly—and the dewy grass will only get my shoes a bit damp.*

So I started off through the field, glorying in the beautiful morning. Soon my shoes and socks were indeed wet. The grass was deeper than I had thought, but it surely wouldn't get any deeper, or so I told myself. I kept going.

After a few more feet, however, I realized the field had a gentle downhill slope to it. The grass that had looked only ankle deep from the parking lot was now up to my knees.

I paused, looking carefully at the several yards of grass I still had to wade through to get to the other side of the field. *Well, it can't get any worse,* I thought. *My shoes, socks and slacks are already drenched. Might as well keep going.*

In less than a dozen steps, however, the ground seemed to disappear and the grass was over my head! I slogged through the ravine, feeling as though I was fighting my way through the jungle in some B grade movie.

But by then I'd gone too far to turn back. The worst was over. A few more steps, and I'd be at the edge of the field and on Lilly Road.

By now I was drenched from head to toe with the heavy dew. But, sure enough, as I plunged ahead, the grass was getting shorter again. It was at my waist, my knees and finally just over my shoes. I was free!

But my rejoicing was short-lived. Just ahead was a deep, mud-filled gully. I stood there for several moments, looking at the muddy slope on the far side that would be impossible to climb up, even if I could safely get down the near side.

In a moment of wild Tarzan fantasy, I surveyed the large tree nearby, looking for a vine on which I could swing over to the other side. Nothing.

I looked back at the grassy field through which I had just come. I didn't want to claw my way through that again. *Surely I can climb this tree somehow and—no, they'll never find my body before spring.*

At this point I could do nothing but turn around and go all the way back through that scary, wet grass. I drove home then but in much worse shape than if I'd taken the long way in the first place.

But some good came out of that experience: Now when I'm tempted to take the easy way out of a situation, I give it another long, hard look first. That invariably takes care of the temptation.

Make Sure You Remarry for the Right Reasons

Millie, a single mom rebounding from her loss, is like a lot of other single gals—she feels better about herself if she has a man by her side. For her, that says, "Hey, I must be doing something right. I've got a man."

What she doesn't see is that he is rude to her and puts her down in front of her friends. She is one of those who's convinced she'll be a good influence on him and will eventually "turn him around."

We play at being a messiah figure. Actually Millie isn't alone. It isn't unusual for women—especially those of us who are doers—to try to fix other people's problems. Doers have to *do.* Not only do we keep trying to correct the mistakes in other people's lives, but we also want to fix *everything.*

That gotta-fix-it mentality is what makes us doers marvelous teachers, social workers, doctors and nurses. Give us a situation that needs fixing, and we'll run through a brick wall if necessary to set things right. Our "we can save the world" mentality has a name: the Messiah Complex.

But the same feelings that compel us to fix everything steer some women into making inappropriate choices in their mates. And we all know women like that—lonely, each one looking for a husband and making the wrong choice, thinking this next guy will surely be the one who will make her life better. *This time*, she tells herself, *everything will be great.*

She's lonely and wondering where the good men are. When she meets someone new, she eventually lets him into her bed in the name of "love" and then winds up feeling used—again.

We are waiting for Prince Charming. In contrast to the would-be Messiah types who seek to rescue men from themselves, too many other single women are waiting to be rescued, convinced they're not whole unless they're half of a pair. But if we're going to wait for someone else—that perfect man—to fulfill all our needs before we can be happy, we'll always be waiting for that mythical person to come along.

Why?

Because no other person can make us whole or complete within ourselves; only God through Christ can do that for us. The truth is that individual self-worth begins with our accepting what the Lord did for us on the Cross.

In the Meantime, What Do We Need to Watch Out For?

When I was in my 20s, I thought gals twice my age were beyond being interested in physical relationships. Well, I'm that age now, and I've discovered even wrinkles and a tired-looking body don't mean the hormones are wrinkled and tired, too. Those little critters are ageless.

But no matter what the movies would have us believe, the world is filled with folks who have learned we *can* control those deep hormonal urgings with the same authority as we control anger. And if we're also wise, we'll discern the difference between the guy who's interested in a serious, ongoing relationship and the guy who's on the prowl for a one-night stand.

So Be Ye Careful and "Be Ye Wise"

In my files, I have an undated clipping from the *Reporter Dispatch* newspaper of Mount Kisco, New York. It reports,

> Men tend to misinterpret female friendliness as a sexual come-on, according to research by psychologist Frank Saal at Kansas State University. In one study, Saal had 200 students respond to a video of a female student asking for an extension on her paper. Women saw the exchange as simply friendly exchange. Saal concludes, "Men tend to over-sexualize what women say and do."

Because I'm naturally outgoing, this matter of how a woman's speech and actions are interpreted is an area I have to watch. People fascinate me—and I love talking to them, telling them my outlandish stories and laughing at theirs. And I'm so thrilled with the joy of this moment—one of the silver linings left over from the School of Hard Knocks—that my friendliness can be misinterpreted, as I discovered when the first guy who asked me out was married.

He was a known womanizer, and I was devastated by his thinking I was *that* type. I tell myself that if anything like that happened *now*, I'd tell him exactly how appalled I was by his invitation. But back then, I merely said I didn't think it would be a good idea, closed the door to my empty classroom and sobbed at the thought of the unwelcome situation—and new world—that singlehood had thrust upon me.

Since then, I've discovered my introduction to the world of womanizers was mild. My friends tell me horror stories of men cooing into the phone, "My wife's visiting her mother. I bet you're lonely, too. Why don't I come over and we can—uh—talk."

Sadly, enough guys meet with enough success using these approaches that they think *all* single women can be won over sooner or later. The only way single women are going to get men to treat them with respect is to demand it with their own high standards.

Beware the Danger of Misunderstood Transference

We single women talk about those unsavory characters we've met, but what about those times when we're attracted not to the womanizer or the wolf on the prowl, but to someone wonderful—the pastor, a coworker or a neighbor?

There's a name for that, too: transference. All the energy and attention that had previously gone into the marriage has to go somewhere, so it's directed toward someone who is not an appropriate recipient.

Misunderstood transference can tempt lonely people into making inappropriate remarks or even into committing adultery. Too often we hear of a pastor who was counseling a distraught woman and then had an affair with her, further complicating her life while destroying his own marriage and ministry.

Unfortunately, that very thing happened with three of my dear friends. When I heard the news, I was personally devastated because previously each one had my utmost respect.

One had an ill wife and started meeting with a mutual friend to pray for her. That friend was a tired, underappreciated young wife who looked forward to their prayer meetings. Soon they were no longer praying but still meeting, and their church was rocked by the scandal.

Another woman worked on a church project with a mutual friend. They'd been friends for years and hadn't *planned* for anything to happen, but it did. He lost his position in the church; she lost her husband's respect, and both would give anything for the affair not to have happened.

Another friend was the office "counselor," and he wanted to help a coworker who was having problems with her ex-husband. It started with kind words, progressed to lunches and culminated in an affair, costing him church leadership and community respect.

Too bad they hadn't read Lois Mowday's excellent book *The Snare: Avoiding Emotional and Sexual Entanglements.* One of the most important things she says:

> If you have a special feeling for another person—and it does happen even with godly, married men and women— subdue it. Don't signal it to that other person. If you keep it to yourself and ask the Lord to help you deal with it, then you are the only one involved. But as soon as you signal to the other person, then he [or she] is involved. This ignites a fire in many people.[1]

Obviously, we don't dare try to fool ourselves by taking even those beginning steps that may lead to immorality.

But Remember That Women Also Can Misread Your Intentions

I remember the moment I was suddenly and sharply reminded of another hazard of being a single mother: being perceived as a threat to the marital happiness of others.

The wife of a colleague let me know in no uncertain terms that she didn't want me working on a project with her husband. She didn't like the way it looked. Actually, she really meant she didn't like the way it looked *to her*.

Her words momentarily left me stunned and speechless. Limp with disbelief at their implications, I sank back into my chair and stared out the window to a beautiful lawn beyond. I may have appeared to be sitting calmly, but I was mentally clawing the air as her words catapulted me into the role of a would-be home-wrecker.

Any strength I had drained away, so I couldn't even respond gracefully "I'm sorry you feel that way" and then leave the room with whatever dignity I could muster.

I've never played the "merry widow," and I'm certainly no predator. Yet I'm not angry with this concerned wife, because she did me a favor. She showed me that I was no longer "Don Aldrich's widow" but "Sandra Picklesimer Aldrich—single woman."

And for that reminder, I'll always be grateful to her.

So What About Dating Again?

Once I'd gotten through the temptation involving Will, the remaining years that were governed by my vow sped by with all the fun and crises of single parenting. Suddenly, both kiddos were in college, so I accepted a coffee date with someone I'd known since fourth grade. And, yes, I was a nervous wreck deciding what to wear and reminding my independent self to wait for him to open the car door.

Now, I occasionally go out for dinner or enjoy an afternoon of exploring Denver antique shops. But I've found that the dating scene has changed too much in the years I've been "off the market." Besides, as I speak around the country, I hear too many horror stories from women who are facing intense pressure to have sex—after only a few dates.

And, in case you're wondering, I've remained celibate all these years. Not only don't I have time for that craziness just yet, but also, at my age, the usual guys who whistle at me are in their 70s and 80s. And somehow, when they blow out their teeth along with the wolf whistle, any romantic effect is lost. Besides, one of the men from church flat out let me know he's looking for a cook and housekeeper! Honey, I write books; I don't dust knick-knacks.

My life is too full now to add one more item to my juggling act. Okay, okay, you may remind me of this when you hear I've run away with some banjo-playing mountain man.

Go Ahead and Date, but Don't Rush to Fill the Void

When I worked on a grief counseling team with Dr. John Canine, a Detroit-area therapist, he was often asked "When is it time to start dating again?" He offered the "three Cs" as guidelines: companionship, common interests and commitment.

As social creatures, we need one another, so dating fills the need, giving us someone to talk to, to be with, to share with. But all too often we jump from companionship to commitment, skipping the important step of common interest.

If the Lord has someone waiting for you, He most likely *won't* send him to ring your doorbell, hand you a dozen roses and say, "Hi, I'm from the Lord." So, it's okay to let your friends know you're ready to date again. Most of your friends and relatives probably have at least one "wonderful guy" for you on their Christmas list.

And who knows? He may *really* be as nice as they say. Just don't rush. And don't skip the common interests connection, including the all-important shared faith.

Take the Initiative, but Be Selective and Sensible

You may have to initiate a few meetings, too. But bypass the local dances and secular singles' clubs. If you want to meet a godly man, look in the places godly people gather. Start by taking part in your church spring cleanups, joining the mission committee or teaching Sunday School. But be careful here, too. At a Florida singles' conference, I was encouraging my audience to be more active in church when a man interrupted me. He then described how guys know churchwomen are "clean." So they attend services just long enough to "scout out the territory" of lonely women and pick up the correct theology phrases that will win her heart—and body. Then he softly added, "I know what I'm talking about. I used to be one of those guys." My jaw dropped in disbelief at this revelation.

If you're not sure you're ready to plunge headlong into the dating scene, you can "test the waters" by talking to men in casual settings. It's amazing how much you can learn about their general philosophies just by asking a simple question in a Sunday School class.

I remember the morning someone used the phrase "normal family," and I innocently asked for a definition. The guy three seats over launched into a tirade, blasting working mothers and condemning Christian counselors. I never got my definition, but I certainly had more than enough information about him.

Set Your Standards; Then Stick Firmly to Them

In my long-ago high school home-economics class, we had a unit on dating. One of the questions was "Should you kiss on a first date?" The purpose of the exercise was to get us to think *before* the date—and thereby set our limits.

Maybe we need to reapply some of that same mentality to our present adult relationships. If you're thinking about dating, do you know what you want in a man? Or will any warm, breathing creature do?

Perhaps my list of what *not* to look for in a man will help you compile your list.

- Never date a man who isn't serious about the Lord.
- Never date a man who doesn't like children, especially yours.

· Never date a man who makes fun of your cultural background, Southern or otherwise.
· Never date a man who is always borrowing money from you.
· Never date a man who says his boss or mother or first wife didn't understand him.
· Never date a man who says you'll never be as good a cook as his mama was.
· Never date a man who calls you by his dog's name.
· Never date a man who drinks—especially if he says he can "handle" his liquor.
· Never date a man who is rude to salespeople or restaurant workers.
· Never date a man who brags about the many "corners" he cut on his income taxes last year.

And my favorite:
· Never date a man who wears a belt buckle embossed with "Hello, Darlin'."

Okay, that's my list of what *not* to look for in a man. And since you know yourself better than I ever could, I'm sure you can draw up your own list of what you do look for in a man. So draw up your list, my friend, but give it some heavy-duty thought and prayer first. And God bless you on your reentry into the dating scene.

So How Do We Handle Our Sexual Needs?

A popular movie shows a brother discovering his sister's battery-operated vibrator during his hunt for a flashlight. I was upset not only by the tackiness of the scene but also at the implication that that's how single women handle their sexual needs.

Many of us have found other and better ways of meeting those needs.

Before some friends decided I was hopeless, they asked if I was "seeing" anybody yet. I knew what they were getting at, so I'd answer them with a quick "I don't have room either in my closets or my life for a man!"

But those who were closest to me would persist. They sometimes even cleared their throats and then asked, "But what about your . . . uh . . . *needs?*"

I'd answer, "I try not to think about them" and promptly change the subject.

I wish I'd had the quotation from the former Colorado Springs pastor Edward K. Longabaugh to help me verbalize my goal: "Sometimes our needs need to take a back seat to the needs of others—not out of weakness but out of the strength Christ has given us."

And, for me, those "others" were my children.

Sublimation Does Work *If* You Redirect Your Thinking

So what *are* singles supposed to do? Various authors have differing ideas, but most agree the only activity that really works is *sublimation.* Rechanneling sexual energy into our work, sports or other wholesome activities results in creative productivity.

In case you're thinking, *Oh, yeah, right!* let me assure you from personal experience that it *is* possible to live a fulfilled life without having a physical relationship.

How?

· By staying out of inappropriate situations
· By not watching movies that will stir up all those old longings

· By not reading inappropriate material
· By staying out of the "Adult Only" corner of the video store
· By working hard and going to bed tired

By pouring energy into other activities, we can smile at ourselves in the mirror and remain genuinely fulfilled.

Sublimation Allows You to Enjoy the Company of Others

A few months into my singlehood, I awakened early one Saturday and couldn't get back to sleep as I remembered long-ago Saturday mornings. Determined to think of other things, I asked myself, *What would you really like to do this summer?*

The most amazing thought bubbled up: *Visit an Old Order Amish family!* With my own farming background, I've long admired the Amish work habits and their careful preservation of the old ways. And perhaps I envy them, too. But whatever my reasons, I'm glad I chose a new adventure instead of dwelling on what I was missing.

Within the next few weeks, through the networking of some friends in Indiana, Jay, Holly and I were invited to the home of a large Amish family. What an amazing day!

Over the next few years, Amish families graciously welcomed the three of us into their homes. The high point of one visit came when the matriarch insisted we stay for the Sunday supper. Twenty-five of us were seated at one wide table filled with hearty dishes I remembered from my own days growing up on a farm.

As I buttered a wheat muffin, I marveled at the long-ago Saturday morning sublimation that had resulted in this wonderful friendship. And I would have missed it entirely if I'd chosen the world's way of releasing sexual tension.

Choose Your Path

Wow, this is another long chapter. But I hope the length reminds you of how important this subject is. Every sexual choice you make today sets you on a specific path for tomorrow. So make sure the path is smooth and peaceful rather than stony and tangled with weeds.

Once More with Feeling

- Whether you remarry is your decision to make. But recognize that your friends and relatives will weigh in on the issue whether you want them to—or not.
- Old friendships can hold new promise. But don't let yourself get burned when old flames rekindle.
- Our self-worth as single mothers begins with accepting what the Lord did for us on the Cross. If we're going to wait for someone else—that perfect man—to fulfill our needs before we can be happy, we'll always be waiting for a mythical person to come along.
- For you, remarriage may be a valid option. But don't let loneliness catapult you into a wrong relationship. If you do remarry, do so for the right reasons.
- Be aware that men tend to oversexualize what women say and do.
- Be aware of the danger of transference. All the energy and attention that had gone into the marriage has to go somewhere. But don't direct it toward someone who is not an appropriate recipient.
- Remember that one of the hazards of being a single mother is being wrongly perceived by another woman as a threat to her own marital happiness.

· When you begin dating again, pray intensely and move cautiously.

· Don't rush to fill the void. As you begin dating again, remember the "three Cs" of a good relationship: companionship, common interests and commitment.

· When entering the dating scene, you may choose to take the initiative, but remain selective and sensible. Set your standards and stick firmly to them.

· If remarriage is not for you, sublimation is. God can meet our needs, not out of weakness, but out of the strength Christ has given us.

· Sublimation does work if we redirect our thinking. Ask yourself what's *really* important. Then find ways to include those things in your schedule.

· Rechanneling sexual energy into work or other wholesome activities results in creative productivity and genuine fulfillment. And you can still enjoy the company and companionship of others.

Note

1. Lois Mowday, *The Snare: Avoiding Emotional and Sexual Entanglements* (Colorado Springs, CO: NavPress,), p. 182.

Guilt, Who Needs It?

If we confess our sins, he is faithful and just and will forgive us
our sins and purify us from all unrighteousness.

1 JOHN 1:9

Guilt and I are old acquaintances. How come? Because, like you, I'm a single mother and I had to work while my children still lived at home. In fact, I still have to work.

Whenever I felt guilty about not being home with my children, I thought about a widow I met at a Kentucky family reunion. Her husband had been injured in the coal mines when he was only 23 —he strained his heart after pushing a loaded coal cart out of the way, she said—and died a couple of years later.

She had no choice but to go to work as a "hired girl" and turn her two- and four-year-old daughters over to her parents to raise. She saw them only once a month for several years.

Like her, most of us don't have a choice either. We have to work.

And with everything else we're handling, we don't need to lay extra guilt on ourselves. Others will do that for us quite readily. So let's just accept the fact that some things are the way they have to be and then grab any extra moment for ourselves and our children that we can!

Three Types of Guilt

I used to think guilt came in only one flavor—the plain vanilla type that told me I could never do enough for my children. But over the years, I've learned it comes in three flavors: true, misplaced and false.

True guilt appears when we've done something wrong and need to ask forgiveness. You know—like when we accuse our child of misbehavior before finding out the entire story.

Misplaced guilt occurs when we blame ourselves for something someone else did. For example, a 12-year-old enjoys riding his bike to and from school each day. We don't think much about it—until he gets hit by a car. Then as his mother sits by the hospital bed, she thinks, *This wouldn't have happened if I'd driven him to school. It's all my fault.* No, it's the fault of the idiot who went through the stop sign.

False guilt often can be identified by the words "should" and "ought." For example, "I should go all out for Christmas to make up for what my children have lost. I'll worry about the bills later." Or "I ought to do all the housework myself since my children have enough challenges in life."

This false guilt is what many of us deal with the most. And it's mean stuff.

Guilt Imposed by Others

I went back to teaching when Jay was less than a year old. And one of the women with whom I worked in the church nursery was always saying in glee, "You're going to miss his first steps."

As Jay began to pull himself up and then work his way across a room by clutching the sofa and chairs, I so dreaded that the sitter—and not I—would witness his first-step milestone that I started to pray about it daily. Somewhere in the middle of my prayers, the thought came that even if I missed those first steps, there'd be plenty of other firsts in which to rejoice.

Then late one afternoon, while I was preparing dinner, 13-month-old Jay worked his way around the kitchen using the walls for support. Suddenly he giggled, let go of the wall and took three big steps right into my open arms.

The following Sunday at church, I had just put on my nursery apron when my coworker stormed in. "I can't believe it!" she snarled. "We went to my cousin's wedding last night and left Becky with a sitter for the first time. And she took her first steps while we were gone."

Amazingly, I felt no glee that what she had wished on me had befallen her.

Guilt Generated by Stereotypes

I also remember one winter afternoon in New York when our company closed early because of an impending storm. I arrived home 30 minutes before Jay and Holly's school bus, so I quickly stirred up a batch of chocolate chip cookies.

I'll never forget the look of surprise on my teens' faces when they opened the door and discovered I was there to greet them. They had barely shaken the snow off their coats when I exclaimed, "And I made cookies! I'm a mom again!"

Even now, that is one of our family jokes. Obviously, I was trying to fit someone else's idea of what "good mothers" are supposed to do. But, as single moms, we can't successfully juggle our responsibilities if we let others heap guilt on our already overburdened shoulders.

Guilt Exploited by Our Kids

Jay and Holly figured out rather quickly that I can handle a crisis but I can't handle guilt. Not only have they used the guilt card whenever it has been to their advantage, but that's also how we got Petey—the tiger cat who took over our household.

For months, Jay and Holly had been asking for a pet, especially since they remembered our previous animals. At first, I patiently explained our schedule, saying it wouldn't be fair to an animal to be left alone so much.

They'd counter that a cat likes being left alone. I again said no.

They described the new litter of kittens in the neighborhood, adding they'd be "put to sleep" if a home wasn't found soon. I remained unmoved.

Finally, Holly looked at me with sorrowful eyes. "How come when we ask you for a kitty, you always say no. But the *first* time we asked Daddy, he said yes?!"

I knew I'd lost. "Go get your cat, Holly."

Both kiddos were out the door almost before I had finished the sentence.

Flex Time or Latchkey Kids?

As single mothers, much of our guilt is caused by the amount of time we must spend away from the children while earning the daily bread. By offering flex-time schedules to working moms, employers greatly lessen our guilt by lessening the time we are away from our kids. And the employers, at the same time, benefit from the improved morale of their employees.

I remember a TV show I saw as a youngster about a pioneer woman and her baby who had been captured by Indians. The

woman begged for the life of her little boy, saying she'd do whatever the warrior wanted if he'd let her son live. He killed the child
anyway.

I left the room, upset and muttering about the man's stu-
pidity. Naturally, the rest of the program would consist of the
trouble the woman would give her warrior-captor for depriving
her of her son.

Even as a child, I understood the principle the warrior had
missed: Let us women take care of what's important to us and
we'll also take care of what's important to our men—male bosses included.

Ask for Flex Time When on the Job

When we moved to New York, my work schedule thrust Jay and
Holly into the world of latchkey kids. I wasn't handling the routine well at all, so I talked it over with my boss. He let me start
my workday earlier so that I could arrive home only an hour later
than my children did. Not only did that greatly help my family
situation, but also the company actually got extra hours out of
me since I often worked through lunch.

Like it or not, Christian women *are* working outside the
home, and Christian organizations in particular should be setting a godly example by offering flexible hours for those who
want them. I'm not looking forward to standing before the Lord
to give an account of my parenting. But I hope I get to ask that
several bosses be made to stand there with me.

Check Out Local Child-Care Possibilities

Most of us get tired enough juggling guilt; we don't need worry
tossed in, too. Child care goes a long way toward alleviating a
working mother's worry—particularly the worry of a mother
with preschoolers—if the child care is good and if the cost is reasonable. If your work site doesn't have a nursery, pray a lot and

look around to see what is available in your area.

Here are a few suggestions worth checking out.

· Is there a church-operated child-care center near you or near your place of work?
· Does your school have an after-school program?
· Do you have older relatives nearby who enjoy spoiling kids and getting paid for it?
· Is there another mother nearby who is staying home with her kids and who would be willing to look after one—or two—more for, say, a monthly fee?
· Can the directors of senior citizens' clubs and organizations—such as the local branch of the American Association of Retired Persons (AARP)—suggest responsible grandparents who could use the extra income and would enjoy the contact with youngsters?
· Do you know any local college students who enjoy kids and can use some extra income?

Make the Kids Safe When They're Home Alone

You can probably think of additional ones, but here are a few ways we can make sure our children are safe at home when we're not there.

Make sure your children are secure and know whom to call in an emergency. Stress the fact that they are never to open the door when they are alone and that they are never to tell a stranger on the phone they're alone.

I always instructed Jay and Holly to say, "I'm sorry, but my mother can't come to the phone right now. If you'll leave a message, I'll have her call you back shortly."

One of the men with whom I taught was angry with me one morning, saying he'd called but Holly wouldn't let him talk to me.

"You couldn't have been in the shower that long!" he snarled, guessing at the reason for Holly's deliberately vague explanation on the phone.

"Oh, you're the one who wouldn't leave his name," I said. And then, though I was under no obligation to tell him, I explained, "I was grocery shopping."

"Well, she could have told me you weren't home."

"Why? She doesn't know you."

"Well, that's dumb."

The other mothers at the lunch table chimed in then, coming to my rescue and letting him know he was really out of line.

Talk to your children about their concerns. Ask them what they hate the most about being home alone and work out ways to make that area less painful.

For Jamie, it was coming into a dark house in the winter. His mother's simple investment in an electric timer took care of the problem.

Make sure your kids have your work phone number. But insist they don't call you to referee their squabbles.

Sharon, now a single mom, remembers the tired mother in the fabric department who got a call right in the middle of cutting a length of material. Sharon could hear her pleading first with one son and then the other, saying she'd help them settle their dispute when she got home in a couple of hours.

Sharon confesses her first thought was *Why doesn't she stay home with her kids where she belongs?* It was easy for Sharon to be self-righteous: Her physician husband paid her bills; their children were cared for a few hours each day by a housekeeper.

When her husband left her for his nurse, Sharon's world came crashing down around her. Eventually, she even had to take a job outside the home. Then she remembered the woman at the fabric shop with a new understanding.

Set up definite rules—including those for chores and visitors. When Jay and Holly were younger, a major rule was that they couldn't have visitors if I wasn't home. Then when we moved to Colorado in their late teens, the rule was occasionally bent—but only if the visitor was of the same gender and if the visitor's parent knew I wasn't home.

The Difficulty of Long, Hot Summers

If at First You Don't Succeed—

Summertime—and the worry is heavy. Yes, summer is an especially tough time for us single moms. Jay and Holly were 14 and 13 the summer after we moved to New York. Several years before, we had purchased a second-hand trailer at a Bible camp on the shores of Lake Michigan. So I sent Jay and Holly back there and arranged for various relatives to stay during the week. I flew or drove back and forth several times during those 10 weeks, further wearing myself out.

The venture was doomed from the start. Several of the women in our lake neighborhood let me know I was robbing my teens. One of the kindest comments was "I think it's terrible you won't be with your children."

At the end of the season, I sold the place—not only to free myself from the financial burden but also to escape the burden of trying to please 40 other mothers.

Try, Try Again

The following summer, I sent Jay and Holly to an inexpensive Christian camp in northern New York for four weeks. I was rather intrigued by the personality dynamics revealed by this experience: Both kids were given the same four-week sentence, but they handled it differently.

Holly was convinced from day one that she wouldn't survive those 28 days. She looked longingly toward home, and thought, *How can I get Mom to get me out of here?* The first postcard I received from her was addressed to "Four Weeks Aldrich." Her subtle humor delighted me, but I was determined she was going to stick it out.

She shrewdly decided next to give me lengthy accounts of how all the campers had to spray their sleeping bags every night to keep the crawling bugs away. The result? I let her come home after serving a two-week sentence: "the longest jail term ever, Mom!"

Meanwhile, Jay looked around and said, "Okay, I'm here for four weeks. What can I do to make it tolerable?"

After I made arrangements to rescue Holly from the crawling things, I told Jay he could come home at the same time.

"No, I'm not going to wimp out," he said.

I stressed that it was okay to come home.

"No, I don't want you to think I'm a wimp like Holly."

"Jay, I won't!"

"Mom, I don't want to see it in your eyes. Just don't do this to me next year."

I didn't.

And Again and Again

The next year, they spent time with relatives back in the Midwest.

Those early teens years are especially troublesome because our children aren't young enough to have a sitter but not old enough to hold a job. I confess, I'm glad to be past that stage.

But if you're still there, pray a lot, talk to other single moms, look into church camps and—most importantly—talk over the situation with trusted relatives, dear friends and your youngsters. These days of summer don't have to sabotage your parenting.

The Importance of Getting On with Life

All of us have situations we wish we'd handled differently. We can't undo those times, but we can learn from them. If you were wrong in some way, confess it to the Lord, ask forgiveness from anyone you've wronged—and then get on with your life.

Let God

I know that little formula sounds easy to follow but, in reality, it is not. We all know it takes some effort. Many people struggle with this concept of letting go and getting on with life, simply because they refuse to accept God's forgiveness for themselves.

At the top of this chapter, I quoted 1 John 1:9: "If we confess our sins, he is faithful and just and will forgive us our sins and purify us from all unrighteousness." So if our almighty, perfect heavenly Father wants to set us free, how can we refuse to accept such freedom? It's ours for the taking.

Guilt can keep us trapped and defeated. And the Enemy loves to have us beat ourselves up emotionally. The devil knows we can't do the Lord's work as long as we concentrate on our failings instead of on the Lord's power to release us from the guilt of failing.

Let Go

I've worked on a professional grief counseling team, but when it comes to dealing with guilt, my mother offers the best advice: "It's like plowing new ground. You can get hung up on a stump root and keep worrying at it all day. Or you can pick up your plow and go on."

I don't know about you, but I'm ready to go on!

Once More with Feeling

- Guilt doesn't come in just plain vanilla—it comes in three flavors: true, misplaced, false. And false guilt is what seems to drive many single mothers.
- We're already handling enough without the extra burden of guilt. Let's make a deliberate effort to accept our situation the way it is and, at least for now, the way it has to be.
- Don't buy it when others try to heap undeserved guilt upon you, and don't exhaust yourself trying to live up to someone else's idea of a "good mother."
- Remember, if our youngsters find us susceptible, they will work the guilt angle any way they can.
- Flexible working hours will reduce the time we are away from our children while on the job. But it's up to each of us to tell our bosses when we need flex-time work schedules.
- Don't forget to explore child-care possibilities that exist in your community, particularly if your kids are preschoolers.
- If your children get home before you do, make sure they are secure and know whom to call in an emergency.
- For older children, set up definite house rules concerning chores and visitors during the times you are at work.
- Summer is an especially tough time for us single moms whose kids are too old for sitters and too young to hold jobs or to remain unsupervised. So start your praying and creative investigations early—with God's grace and your forethought, you can plan for how your kids will spend those long, hot summers.

- We can't change the past, but we can learn from it. Confess past wrongs, accept God's forgiveness and then let go of them.
- When we concentrate on our failings instead of on the Lord's power and grace to free us from the guilt of failure, we're playing right into the Enemy's hands. Accept God's freedom from the trap of guilt, and get on with your life.

Keep 'Em Talking and Keep Listening

Rejoice with those who rejoice; mourn with those who mourn.

ROMANS 12:15

Rain had fallen for several days on President Thomas Jefferson and his party as they traveled cross-country on horseback. In their journeying, they reached the river they were to cross and found the rain-swollen waters had swept away their only bridge.

The president and his entourage meandered up and down the riverbank for a while until they discovered a place where their horses could safely take them across. Nearby, a man sat hunched under a tree. He stood up as he saw the group approach.

Then he spoke to President Jefferson. "Please, sir, will you carry me across the river with you?"

President Jefferson nodded and helped the man swing up behind him. When they arrived safely on the far bank, the man jumped down and offered his thanks.

One of Jefferson's escorts turned to the now-dismounted rider and challenged him. "How is it you dared to ask to ride behind the President of the United States?"

The man blanched, looked into the kind face of his benefactor and then faced his questioner. "I didn't know I was speaking to the President," he said. "It's just that I saw no in your faces and yes in his."[1]

Kids Will Communicate When We Moms Are Approachable

That's what communication with our children is all about—making sure they see *yes* in our faces and know we *are* approachable. Despite our intense schedules, we must work to create a nonjudgmental atmosphere in which our sons and daughters can safely say what is on their minds.

We all know the things that say *no* to teens: put-downs, sarcasm, orders, "you should" statements and impatience that cuts them off in midsentence.

So what makes for approachability?

Offer Sincere Compliments

True, sometimes we have to say no. But even then we don't need to be unnecessarily negative or overly critical. Kids aren't going to listen to what we're saying if our facial expressions as well as our words announce our disapproval of everything they do. Most kids really do want to do it right.

When I interviewed the late West Coast counselor Jean Lush, she said that when she worked with her father she felt as though she could do anything. He told funny stories, offered lavish praise and made his four children feel as though they were the greatest in the world. Her mother, however, was frustrated by their fumbling efforts and often compared them to their Aunt Ida, the family misfit.

Guess which parent's requests were answered with enthusiasm?

Mrs. Lush also liked to remind single moms that many of the world's great leaders and scientists were raised only by their mothers.

A welcome thought!

Keep Them Talking

Just because children don't talk doesn't mean they aren't hurting. In fact, those may be the very ones who are carrying the greatest pain.

Find ways to spend one-on-one time together. You might even come up with the rule that they must take turns helping you prepare dinner. Working together forces us to talk.

But don't expect to solve all of life's problems with one intense conversation. The human mind often has to consider a thought, talk about it, put it aside and then talk about it again.

Chris said that after her divorce, her sons were relieved that their father's abuse had come to an end, so they refused to talk at first. But gradually over the next year, they needed to sort through it all again—and taking a short walk each evening after dinner gave them that opportunity.

Keep the Questions Coming

Even when Jay and Holly were toddlers, our favorite after-dinner activity was a walk around the block. I often peppered those times with my "What would you do if" questions.

When they were four and five, the questions were basic protection: "What would you do if you were playing in our front yard, and a man stopped and asked you to come over to his car?"

As they got older, the questions progressed to whatever they might be dealing with in school: "What would you do if your best friend forgot to study for the history test and asked you to keep your paper uncovered?"

One Sunday, when my kids were 11 and 12, I impulsively asked, "What do you wish I'd do differently?"

Holly shrugged a "nothing."

But Jay immediately had a suggestion. "I wish you liked science more."

I nodded. "I wish I did, too. But we both know that isn't going to happen anytime soon. Meanwhile, how 'bout if we get a membership at the Cranbrook Science Museum?"

That proved exactly the right thing to do. Every few weeks, we'd meander past the latest displays, while Jay explained what we were seeing. Occasionally, I even understood enough to enable me to ask an intelligent question.

I never did get excited about molecules and atoms, but it was important to Jay—and, thus, important to me.

Once Jay and Holly hit their teens, my questions got even more specific: "What would you do if you were at a party and someone offered you a joint? What would you do if your date said his/her parents were away for the weekend and suggested you go over there?"

By the way, they never had to run from the stranger in the car, but they were asked to cheat, were offered joints and were propositioned.

I'm grateful they handled the situations well. I know it was God's mercy and answered prayers that got them safely through, but the tired single mother in me still likes to think that some of our early game-playing with questions paid off.

Don't Go Looking for Battles

At 17, Jay let his blond hair grow to his shoulders, and he

couldn't be bothered with the current styles. His favorite casual outfit consisted of faded jeans and a Hawaiian shirt. When he had to attend formal school functions, he usually wore his Scottish kilt.

Just as he entered his "Scottish stage," he discovered an antique wood carving of a rugged clansman wrapped in a tartan. Hanging over one shoulder was a single, long braid.

As soon as Jay showed me the carving, I knew what he planned to do. "I don't care if you grow your hair to your knees," I said. "Just keep it clean."

He was active in the youth group and still attending the worship service, so I didn't think much more about it. But as the months wore on, I realized *I* was being judged for Jay's long hair.

Single moms have enough spiritual battles without accepting false ones, so I shrugged off the comments of the questioning adults with, "Actually, if my hair was the color of Scottish gold, I'd grow it out, too." (Besides, I knew his closest male relatives had balded early, so I wanted him to enjoy having hair for as long as he could.)

But the most frustrating comments came from some Bible colleges that called to invite Jay to the campus for the day. As soon as Jay would tell them about the length of his hair, their first question to him *wasn't* "Do you want to know more about the Lord?" but "Are you willing to cut your hair?"

Isn't it a pity we live in a world of outward appearances? We lose more youngsters that way—by trying to make them into clones of ourselves instead of helping them discover who they are in Jesus.

Anyway, Jay finally decided to attend a state university renowned for its chemistry department. Then, that decision made, he promptly cut his hair! When I questioned him about it, he merely shrugged. "It's time," he said.

So, Mom, take heart and don't do battle over unimportant things. Battle drugs and alcohol, not length of hair, neatness of rooms or choice of music—unless it's obscene.

And say yes as often as possible; it gives more credibility to the times when you must say no.

Dr. Dobson tells about the waitress who had explained to him that she and her 12-year-old daughter were battling because the youngster wanted to shave her legs. They'd had a miserable year because of that raging discussion, and the mother didn't know what to do.

What would the famous psychologist suggest?

Dr. Dobson looked at her and said, "Buy her a razor!"

⚲Do Get Their Response
Make sure your youngsters understand what you mean as well as what you say.

Carol learned early that her son can't be bothered by the mundane and tunes her out when she's giving him instructions. She now asks him to repeat what she has asked him to do. Otherwise, she found she'd say, "You have a dentist appointment this afternoon. Come home right after school." Then he'd answer, "Okay" without knowing what he'd agreed to.

Kids Will Communicate When We Moms Listen

Hear Them Out
Hearing our kids out means we must really listen to what they are trying to say to us. They need to know we are listening.

Most of us are so intent on what we want to *say* that we don't listen. We're merely waiting our turn to speak. This is especially true when we're trying to impart our vast, hard-earned wisdom to our teens. *If only they'd listen,* we think, *they wouldn't suffer the same consequences.*

So, yes, we must do our share of the listening. Youth speakers emphasize that many teens are sexually promiscuous because they're trying to connect with someone. If they had people willing to listen to them, these experts say, the teens wouldn't be reaching out in inappropriate ways.

So set a good example. If you expect them to listen to you, you've got to listen to them.

Empathize with Them

Remember what worked for you when you were younger. Most of us learned through our mistakes. Why? Because, even when our parents tried to warn us, most of us thought we were being lectured. And we ended up learning a lot the hard way.

One single mother told me the lines of communication with her 16-year-old daughter opened the evening she realized how her talks must have sounded to a teen. The turning point came as she quietly said, "Where you're going, I have been."

One of my recurring themes—as a teacher and later as a mother and speaker—continues to be: "These are *not* the best years of your life! It *will* get better—if you'll let it." Then I remind my listeners that wrong choices about drugs, alcohol, friends and sexual activity can threaten a bright future. Teens always seem relieved when I assure them a brighter future awaits, but invariably one of them asks, "So why do our folks always say these are such great years?"

The obvious answer is that teens have choices. The older we get, the more limited our choices become. But in an emotional moment, adults often have trouble verbalizing that fact.

I've reached the stage in life where I truly understand the old saying "Youth is wasted on the young." But the only thing I miss about my youth is the firm skin. I still wouldn't want to go through all those crises again.

Share Their Concerns

Just before Jay's sixteenth birthday, he asked about the Vietnam War. I'd worked as a civilian secretary for a Reserve Officers' Training Corps (ROTC) unit at the end of the war, so I answered his questions by sharing my experiences with him. I told him about the hippie era and my own conservative denial of the reality of war until Clive, the handsome senior I remembered from my high school study hall, came home in a body bag.

But I still couldn't fully describe the craziness of that era or what it was like for our soldiers, not knowing who the enemy was. Finally, I decided to take him to see *Good Morning, Vietnam*. The movie was rated R, but I took a deep breath and escorted him. With far greater impact than I ever could have had, the scenes explained both the air of distrust that prevailed then and the Army's own way of handling things.

Later, over soft drinks, I tried to answer his remaining questions. When I mentioned that three of my classmates had died in the war, he asked for specifics about them. I described Clive's future ambitions and Bob's quickness on the football field.

Then I talked about Scott. He was two years behind me in high school. I remember the morning I first saw him as I came out of the cafeteria. He stood near the atrium with a shaft of sunlight falling on him, looking first at his schedule and then down the hallway in bewilderment. I directed him to the proper hallway and went on my way—never to think about the scene again until I heard about his death several years later. For weeks, I was tormented by the news. Even now I wonder if he'd stood in a patch of sun, looking around in that same bewildered way, with no one to direct him away from the snipers or land mines.

Even after our long talk, Jay still had questions. I could have introduced him to the war section of our local library, but since we lived just a few hours from Washington, D.C., I decided the three of us would drive down to see the Vietnam Veterans Memorial.

How do I describe the sight of the wall with the names of more than 56,000 young men and women who were killed trying to defend something they didn't understand?

Near the main sidewalk, two middle-aged vets looked up names in the thick directory they carried.

Close by, a scoutmaster had a disinterested youngster by the lapels saying, "Some of them were my friends. Someday you'll understand what you've seen here."

Fathers held up toddlers so they could touch a name, whispering, "No, put your hand just a little higher. There! That's your grandpa."

I wept as I thought of that toddler's grandfather who had probably been in his early 20s when he had died, leaving behind a son who was little older than the child he now held up.

As we walked away from the wall, Jay shyly looked at me. "Thanks, Mom," was all he said.

I put my arm around his shoulders. "No, honey, thank *you.*"

Take Their Problems Seriously

With all we're juggling emotionally, physically, spiritually, mentally and financially, we can be tempted to shrug at what our children see as problems—whether it's uncooperative hair or having to eat lunch alone at school when a best friend is sick.

Every time we dismiss present petty problems, we're closing the door of communication on future problems as well. Jenna's 11-year-old daughter chattered constantly, telling her every detail of the school day, including what her friends wore for gym class, what they ate for lunch and what they talked about in the halls.

After one particularly long day, Jenna didn't know if she could listen to one more account of who spilled chocolate pudding on the cafeteria floor. But she determined that if she still wanted her daughter to talk to her when she was dating at 16, she'd better listen to the pudding accounts *now.*

Finally, Jenna said, "Let's take turns, okay? You tell me every-thing that happened in gym class in 15 minutes, and then it's my turn to tell you—in 15 minutes—everything that happened at work today."

Not only did the exchange give Jenna a chance to vent her own disappointment over not being invited to a briefing meet-ing, but it also gave her daughter a glimpse of the hassles her mother was dealing with every day.

Get to Know Their Friends

Want your kids to tell you what's going on at school? Then ask with whom they eat lunch, who their teachers are and who's on their bus. Yes, that takes effort, but school takes up most of their day, and their peers take up most of their thoughts.

Melinda said she was terrified when she met some of her son's friends at a school play. She'd known her son didn't care about his wardrobe, but she wasn't expecting the wild hair, the army surplus coats and the holey jeans his friends wore.

Melinda had the good sense not to demand he get new friends; instead, she invited them all over for pizza and colas after the play. She's still not happy with the way they all dress, but at least she's confident they aren't a drug gang.

Recently she ran across a photo of herself as a high school student and says the sight of her straight hair, white lipstick, miniskirt and go-go boots reminded her that teens do survive even wild fashions.

And Stay Friends with Your Own

Dr. James Dobson's advice about parenting teens is right on the mark: "Just get them through it."

I've found that teens will test us constantly. And it's a tough ball for us to juggle with everything else. But when our teens test us, they are really asking, "Do you love me?"

And we can't assume our teens hear our quiet pronouncements. As difficult as it is for us to do sometimes, we must constantly say, "Yes, I love you," and say it repeatedly through a quick hug, a pat on the shoulder and—dare I say it again?—by *listening* to them as well as by talking and talking.

Be Careful What You Say When Talking About the Other Parent

Don't Belittle the Other Parent

Widows are often tempted to tell their children only the good qualities about their father. One of my friends did it too well—her son refused to play football, thinking he'd never be as good as his dad.

Divorced moms have to fight the other temptation: to talk only about the undesirable qualities of the ex-spouse. But children of divorced parents often are struggling with guilt and loss of self-esteem, so it's important that we not add to their emotional struggles by belittling the other parent.

Diane handled this situation beautifully with her 15-year-old son when she introduced him to me. As we chatted, he said, "Some people think I look like my mother. But I don't think so, do you?"

Before I could answer, Diane smiled and said, "No, you look like your dad."

Then she turned to me. "His dad is a fox! That's why I married him."

As her son smiled shyly, I thought about Diane's bitter divorce and marveled at the fact that she didn't transfer that pain onto her son with a sarcastic comment about his looks. Instead, her words were an incredible gift of self-esteem.

And Don't Transfer Blame

Renee, to this day, is convinced she caused her parents' marriage to fail. She still remembers the evening she timidly approached her crying mother with, "Why did Daddy leave?"

In return, Renee heard only, "Everything was fine until you came along!"

If nothing else, let's determine to bite back those stinging comments and concentrate on getting through the days ahead. This restraint is especially important if the child spends weekends with the noncustodial parent.

When Clarie packed her two children's overnight bags for the first weekend with their dad, she literally put a piece of masking tape over her mouth to keep her from saying all the bitter things she was thinking.

"My son and daughter thought it was a game and put tape on their mouths, too," she says. "We all looked pretty silly, but it helped me get through the packing."

Most Important of All: Pray with Your Children

One of my favorite childhood memories is of my Kentucky grandparents, Papa and Mama Farley, kneeling by their living room chairs each evening and praying aloud at the same time. I'd try to pray, too, but I was so intrigued by the thought of God sorting their voices I'd never get through my own petitions.

I wonder what memories of prayer Jay and Holly have carried into their adulthood. I'd like it to be of the prayers and Scripture after dinner, but it probably is the times of crisis when I began with, "Lord, you know I hate days like this."

Connie says her mother's prayers followed her all over Southern California during the '60s hippie era.

"No matter where I was or what I was doing, I knew she was praying for me," Connie says. "The memory of her kneeling next to her bed with the Bible open just wouldn't leave me. Now that

I'm raising my daughter alone, I'm trying to teach her to talk to God just as easily as she talks to me. And that means she has to see me doing it, too."

But what if praying with another person is new to you?

You take a deep breath for courage and tell your children you'd like them to join you in talking to God together. Sometimes, though, you don't have time to have the family discussion first.

Vina had always felt awkward about praying aloud, too, but when her teen daughter threatened to move out, she remembered the comfort her friend's prayers gave her in a crisis. Impulsively, she wrapped her daughter in a bear hug and prayed aloud, "Lord, help me show this special little gal I really do love her. Amen."

They hugged for a moment and then the daughter pulled back to look at her mother. "How come you've never prayed with me before?"

At Vina's stammered, "I guess I was afraid," the daughter hugged her again. Finally they were communicating on a level the teen could understand.

Remember, You're Being Watched

I recall the evening I was especially troubled about a looming decision, so I retreated to my bedroom to read the Word and jot down verses that spoke to my dilemma. I picked up the old white Bible on my nightstand. A couple of other Bibles were there, newer translations, but this was the Bible I'd had since the seventh grade. The verses were underlined, the margins written in, the cover worn. Now I searched through the worn pages for an answer to my latest challenge.

Within a few minutes, then ten-year-old Jay came up the stairs looking for me. Nine-year-old Holly intercepted him in the hallway.

"Don't bother Mom," she whispered. "She's reading the Bible—her *white* one."

I heard Jay exclaim, "Oh!" and go back downstairs. I hadn't realized anyone noticed which Bible I read when I was the most troubled. But our children, even at a young age, observe far more than we think they do. Yes, that can be an unsettling thought. But our actions impact our kids more than the most eloquent lecture ever could. And, like it or not, they will follow our example. Let's make sure it's a good one.

Once More with Feeling

- Your children will communicate with you when they see *yes* in your face and know you *are* approachable.
- Stay positive and be free with praise as you encourage them to talk to you.
- Dare to ask questions, but don't go looking for battles.
- Say yes as often as possible; it gives more credibility to the times when you must say no.
- Get their response to be sure your youngsters understood what you meant as well as what you said.
- Youth may truly be wasted on the young, but their struggles are real. So listen to what your kids are saying and let them know you empathize with them.
- Set a good example for your children. If you expect them to listen to you, you must listen to them.
- Share their concerns and take their problems seriously.
- Stay friends with your kids and get to know their friends.
- Be careful what you say about their other parent. Don't belittle and don't transfer blame. He may be your ex-husband, but he's still their father.

· Most important of all, pray with your children. Not only are you wrapping them in God's protection and guidance, but you're making comforting memories.

Note

1. Dr. John Stevens (sermon given at First Presbyterian Church, Colorado Springs, CO.)

Guiding Our Teens Through Sexual Waters

No temptation has seized you except what is common to man.
And God is faithful; he will not let you be tempted beyond what you
can bear. But when you are tempted, he will also provide a way out
so that you can stand up under it.

1 CORINTHIANS 10:13

Just before Holly's thirteenth birthday, I discovered the oldest son of one of my friends was in prison for car theft. When I called to encourage the boy to attend the classes the prison chaplain offered, he told me he had fathered a child when he was only 15!

Argh! Jay and Holly dreaded my hearing about some teen getting pregnant: they knew they would have to hear the "I'm-tough-for-a-reason" lecture. That time was no different, but only Holly was home at the moment. As I finished telling about the situation, I'd said that when she started dating, I'd have to meet each date before the big event and if I didn't like him, she wasn't going out with him.

She rolled her eyes and muttered I'd forgotten what it was like to be a teen. I pounced on her words.

"No, Holly. I'm tough because I *do* remember."

We Can Get Through the Teen Years Intact

These times of sexual permissiveness and low moral standards are frightening for parents of teens. But we can't hide our heads in the sand and ignore the fact that so many young lives today are disrupted and even ruined in a few moments.

In my first year of teaching in Michigan, two delightful 15-year-old students in my first-hour English class created a baby. To this day, they both wonder about the child they placed for adoption. Other students went away for long weekends to get abortions—and turned to drugs and/or alcohol to deaden the emotional pain. Time after time, I had girls crying at my desk after school, telling me they were pregnant.

One year, a sophomore told me, "But I don't think I'm *really* pregnant. We did it for just a couple of seconds." Another year I remember a senior telling me she'd only "done it" one time. But one time was all it took.

The girls and I would talk, and I'd offer to go with them to tell their parents, but no one ever took me up on that offer. I wish I'd given more hugs along with my words of comfort, but after they'd leave, *I'd* cry.

Though I was no longer the concerned teacher when my kids were teens, I was a mom who had to be careful that my memories of those students and my fears didn't cloud my own children's dating.

Of course, it's tough trying to keep our teens on the straight and narrow. And, I confess, the best years for me as a single mom were when Jay was 15 and Holly 14—because he couldn't drive and she couldn't date!

But this challenging time doesn't have to overwhelm us—as long as we keep our own standards high and keep talking to our teens about theirs. And it doesn't matter what their friends' parents say. I remember one mother who decided her own sexual activity as a teen limited any advice she could offer about abstinence. So when her teens started dating, she bought a large, clear glass cookie jar and filled it with brightly colored condoms, saying only she'd replenish the supply as needed. What a horrible message.

We are the parents, and it's up to us to provide the guidance our teens need—and want. And we can't leave this area to the school professionals either. After all, the only "safe sex" is no sex. The rates of sexually transmitted infections are alarming despite the promises of so-called experts. And these modern infections are not the ones of past generations that were cured with a shot or two of penicillin. HIV, AIDS, herpes, genital warts—associated with HPV, which causes cervical cancer—are just a few of the infections awaiting new homes.

We Need to Answer the Unasked Questions

For far too many single parents, their own sex education consisted of a horrified mother clutching at her blouse and reeling backward in mortification when asked embarrassing questions. Too often, the one caution offered the girls was a mysterious "Be careful. Boys are after only one thing."

That universal warning really worried me because I didn't know what it was they were after. I knew I didn't have any *money*.

Thus, as a single mom, I tried to stress to my teens that sexual feelings are normal and, in fact, God-given, but are to be controlled until marriage. And, I insist, those feelings *can* be controlled.

When adults say, "Be careful your feelings don't run away with you," they're conveying the idea that sexual feelings are so strong that they can overrule judgment. That's an incorrect message to give.

Our sexual feelings are really no different from our other feelings, such as anger and jealousy. Just as we don't have to act on our anger, neither do we have to act on our sexual feelings. And I tried to stress that point to Jay and Holly, both in our discussions and in visible reminders. Just about the time they hit puberty, I put a 3"x5" card on their desks with this message: "You may not be able to control your feelings, but you *can* control your actions."

What Is Going On in His Mind?

One issue single mothers are often reluctant to discuss with their sons is masturbation. One thing that helped me to prepare for such a discussion was Father's Night for the dads of the sixth-grade boys at Jay's school in Michigan. I'd been single for two years, so *I* attended, sitting in the midst of all those fathers who were trying to ignore a lone woman.

The Statistic
The counselor talked about puberty and gave me helpful insights—including the statistic that 98 percent of all teen boys masturbate and the other 2 percent lie about it. Maybe those 2 percent really do believe it will grow hair on their palms.

Years ago, Charlie Shedd, in his book *The Stork Is Dead*, encouraged parents to consider masturbation as a gift from God—a way to release the tension. Those of us helping with the youth group had used the book for group discussion and were encouraged (and occasionally shocked) by the resulting frank discussions. The group's parents were upset, though, saying we were putting thoughts into their teens' heads and that our church was not the place for such explicit material.

The Controversy

One summer on our way back to visit relatives in Michigan, I retold the episode to Jay and Holly, including the problem we'd had over that particular chapter. Then I quoted the counselor's humorous statistics about the number of males who masturbate, and I added the comments from those long-ago frantic parents ranging from "Jesus wouldn't have done that!" to "I'm pulling my child out of youth group!"

Then I ended with this thought: "I agree with Charlie Shedd. If occasional masturbation works as a release valve and keeps a young person out of sinful dating situations, then I think it's okay. It's far better to rechannel energy into sports or work, but I've never been a teen boy, so things are undoubtedly more intense for them than I can know. The real problem comes with what's going on in the mind during those few moments."

With the miles rolling under our wheels, I told them about the summer when I organized a drama class for teens at the now-defunct psychiatric hospital in Eloise, Michigan. "One young man—a freshman in college—was there because his masturbation habit had taken over his entire life."

Jay chuckled. "See? They're right when they say it makes you insane."

I laughed at his attempt to lighten the moment, then said, "Actually, he was overwhelmed by stress and had mistakenly identified the source of that stress as being sexual. He masturbated 10 to 12 times a day. Finally his roommates convinced him he had to talk to the college psychiatrist. He wound up in the hospital so that he could get the help he needed."

Then I realized the story, meant just as an interesting aside, wasn't supporting my original premise that normal masturbation is, well, normal. I added that if they had any questions in the future, I'd be happy to discuss it further.

The Problem

Jay turned toward me. "How'd you answer those parents? *Do* you think Jesus masturbated?"

Sometimes my brain actually hurt as I tried to sort through their questions.

"Well, Jay, the Bible says in Hebrews 4:15 Jesus was tempted just as we are, but didn't sin," I said. "So to answer that, we have to decide first of all whether masturbation is a sin.

"The problem, of course, is what goes on in the mind during the act. I'm convinced Jesus kept a pure thought life so, to answer your question, I guess He didn't. Kind of contradicts what I said earlier, huh?"

As Jay nodded in his forgiving way, Holly asked about the other students in the class that summer. I was only too happy to stroll down a different part of memory lane as the car rolled toward Michigan.

Stress the Goal of No Regrets Later

I had been invited to a college spiritual retreat to speak on the topic of "Finding God's Will." I went prepared with Scriptures and principles such as "God's direction for today never contradicts His Word" and "His call will be persistent." But the weekend proved to be an eye-opener for me; I hadn't expected to hear so many confessions from Christian young people.

On the second night we were there, one of the girls sat on my bunk and sobbed her story of sexual activity, saying, "I want to go back to the way I was."

Another one young woman told me her boyfriend had broken up with her after their intimacy. His reason? He was disappointed that *she* hadn't been stronger.

My friend Rose is often called on to give talks to youth groups. Once she was speaking at a church in Alta Loma, California, and she was driving home the point that the teens needed to make good choices now so that they wouldn't have regrets later on.

Just at that moment, in one of those marvelous coincidences, the assistant pastor walked into the room and stood quietly in the back. Startled at seeing him, she stared at him for a moment; then, in bewilderment, she called him by name.

He looked just as stunned at seeing her. "Rosie?" he queried in surprise.

To her startled audience she said, "Back in Romulus, Michigan, more than 30 years ago, I dated your pastor. How would we have felt just now at seeing each other again if we had been intimate back then?"

Plan Ahead for the Dating Years

A few months after Holly's twelfth birthday, she asked when she could start dating. I wanted to clutch my blouse and reel backward. But instead, I calmly asked, "When do you think would be a good time to start?"

She thought for a moment, and then she said, "I think 16 is a good age."

I wasted no time. "That's a good idea, Holly. Why don't we write that down, along with a few other thoughts."

The Contract

So we dutifully drew up what would later be known as the Contract. We sat at the dining room table in our Michigan home and discussed several situations. Then she carefully printed the following rules.

- At 14½, the start of freshman year, a boy can come over to do homework.
- At 15, a parent drives for group dates.
- No "real" dates until 16. Curfew will be 11:00 P.M. or time agreed to by Mom and Holly.
- No kissing until 16 for Big Party of Holly's choice.
- No going steady until college.
- No getting engaged until Holly's senior year in college.
- No marriage until Holly's college degree is complete.
- Rules may be added to this list.

Holly wrote the date at the top of the paper and then we both signed it. I folded it and put it in a safe place. I'd just bought myself several years of peace—or so I thought.

The Resistance

Everything was going along just fine until we were living in New York. To hear my daughter tell it, every girl in Fox Lane Middle School was going steady by the time she was in eighth grade. When she'd insist that she, too, be allowed to date, I'd calmly ask, "What does the Contract say, Holly?"

More than once she stomped out of the room, muttering, "I'm never signing anything again."

Somehow we got through middle school, but I dreaded the approach of her fifteenth birthday when she could group date. Sure enough, it wasn't long after her birthday that she and a young man from her class were the sweethearts of first-hour lunch.

I insisted upon meeting him before they could go bowling with the rest of their friends. He had the good sense to be nervous, but he gave me details of where they were going, which parent would drive and when they'd return. I took a deep breath, knowing the next step was just around the corner.

The Pressure

In the months that followed, I could see from Holly's tension that she was being pressured. The young man had known about Holly's determination that she wouldn't kiss until after her sixteenth birthday since she wanted her big party. But he thought he could change her mind. And he was starting to display hostility toward me and the Contract, saying I had tricked Holly into signing something at 12 that had no relevance to the real world, and that I was being too strict with her.

The Discussion

One afternoon, I came home late with my briefcase packed with articles to be reworked by the next morning. But Holly was aggravated, so I ignored the work. For the next hour and a half we talked about present decisions affecting future relationships.

Holly informed me that the normal procedure in her school was for the guy to ask the girl out for their first date, and then they'd kiss. She insisted she had waited all those months and was tired of having a "dumb contract" forcing her to wait.

"Fine, Holly," I finally said. "If you want to kiss him, go ahead. But remember, the deal was I'd pay for a Sweet Sixteen party only if it *is* a Sweet Sixteen party. Life's full of decisions. You can't have everything. Make your choice."

The Decision

Believe it or not, she chose the party and asked him not to pressure her anymore. I'd like to report that he was really impressed by her attitude and told her he respected her for making such a decision. But alas, he broke up with her and started dating her best friend.

Still, just before her party, she received so much attention from several guys who knew about her rule that she panicked. One young man even sent her an incredible bouquet of flowers, hoping to be chosen as her escort for the evening. But by then she was feeling special and chose not to pair off with one guy.

The Caution

The night after the flowers arrived, I had gone to bed at about 11 P.M. Holly was on the phone, so I called a "cut it short" to her and pulled the quilt around my shoulders. I fell into a deep sleep, yet I had the most disturbing dream that Holly was in her room, picking snakes up from the floor. She'd hold them up, examine them, let them writhe over her hands.

I woke up then, in a cold sweat, my heart pounding from the intensity of the dream. I looked down the hallway and could see a light from under her door—even though it was after midnight.

I found her still on the phone. I motioned for her to sign off. Then I sat on the bed and asked why she was still up. She explained her old boyfriend had called.

Suddenly my nightmare made sense. I told her about it, and ended with, "Holly, be careful whom you date. Don't play with snakes."

The Resolution

She didn't date him again, and the phrase "Don't play with snakes" quickly became one of our family codes.

Now I realize this story sounds old-fashioned, but not every teen out there is sexually active. Recently, in fact, the beautiful daughter of a friend showed me her "promise ring" that reminds her of her vow not to have sex before marriage and not to do drugs or drink. By the way, the teens of this decade are not the only ones who have ever faced sexual pressure. Nor are they the discoverers of such activity. And though they may not verbalize it, they need—and want—protection in that scary new world. Remember, we are the parents. It's up to us to provide guidance.

Ask to Meet the Dates

Shortly after we moved to Colorado, one of the guys on the wrestling team asked Holly to go bowling. I had hoped to put off the Talk a few more months, but there he was—a handsome young man with a neck like a tree trunk, asking to take my daughter out.

The Talk

The Talk consisted of Holly's would-be date having to answer a series of questions about his interests, previous residences and family background.

This young man was nervous and kept glancing toward the stairway, wondering when Holly would be ready.

I smiled. "It's okay. She'll be downstairs when this is over."

I gestured toward the window where we could see his blue car parked in front of the house. I uttered the typical challenge of a concerned parent: "That's a nice car. Obviously, you take good care of it. But what would you do if a stranger came to your door one evening and asked if he could borrow it, even adding he'd take good care of it."

The lad smiled in sudden understanding. "I'd tell him I'd have to know him better."

I nodded. "Exactly. And you've shown up here, asking to take my daughter out for the evening. Her value is far more precious to me than your car to you.

"But even though we've met, I still don't know much about you. Right now you think this is ridiculous, but I guarantee in a few years when a stranger comes to your door to borrow your daughter for the evening, you'll think of me and say, 'That ol' lady was right!'"

I let that thought sink in. Then I continued. "Another thing: You two are just going out as friends, but I've lived long enough to know how quickly situations can change. So remember this, treat Holly the way you hope some other guy is treating your future wife."

His eyes widened. I knew I'd hit my target and won the round.

The Benefit

Only one young man refused to meet with me, so Holly told him not to call her again. "It's like my mom says, 'You don't have to like it; you just have to do it,'" she said.

She later confessed she was glad I had the rule because the guy had made her nervous. Of course, I appreciated her comment, but it also underscored the fact she was depending on my in-charge parenting as her protection.

Recognize That Prayer Has More Power Than Talking

Yes, in case you're wondering, I met Jay's dates, too, but usually over lunch at our home and without the tension. Reluctant to have "good ol' Mom" chauffeur him and a date, he had decided to hang out with various girls through the youth group activities until he had his driver's license.

And I didn't terrorize the girls in the same way I had the wrestlers. Instead, I talked to my son about his responsibility in a dating setting. Amazingly, though, those talks with the guys who wanted to date Holly were almost easy compared to the private conversations I had with Jay. I remember the days when mothers had to teach their daughters to say no. Well, today's mother is having to teach her *son* to say no.

I confess, at times part of me longed for the day when Jay and Holly would be adults, and I won't have to be so watchful. But my older friends laughed, telling me my job wouldn't be over even then. "You just wait until your children turn into grandchildren," they'd say.

Argh!

But over the years, I learned that my prayers carry more power than my talking. So, believe me, I prayed *a lot* then—and continue that necessary practice.

Like those long-ago parents who argued against sexual discussions in our church youth group, I wanted to pretend my teens were above such temptations, but I knew better. We single moms may not get through this as well as we'd like, but by talking to our children—and the Lord—and being ever watchful, we increase our chances of raising our children to make sound moral choices.

And isn't that our goal?

Once More with Feeling

- You can get through this time if you keep your standards high and keep talking to your teens about theirs.
- Answer the unasked questions. Often children need you to anticipate and answer those questions they can't verbalize.
- Sexual feelings don't have to be acted on. Actions can be controlled even when feelings cannot be.
- Counselors tell us that 98 percent of all teen boys masturbate and the other 2 percent lie about it.
- Stress to your teens the goal of living their lives now in such a way that they won't have regrets later.
- Plan ahead for the time when your teens will be dating. Know what you are going to say and do.
- Work out rules with your teens governing their dating

and then write them down. Written contracts save untold hassles.

· Teens of this decade are not the only ones who have ever faced sexual pressure. And though they may not verbalize it, they need—and want—protection in that scary new world.

· Meet your teen's dates before the event.

· Remember that prayer has more power than talking, so pray—a lot!

Battling the Bills and Winning the War

Better a little with the fear of the LORD than great wealth with turmoil.
Better a meal of vegetables where there is love than a fattened calf with hatred.

PROVERBS 15:16-17

I have in my files a copy of a letter from a single mother, which arrived at the Focus on the Family office shortly after one of my appearances on the daily broadcast.

It begins, "Dear Dr. Dobson, I really resent Sandra Aldrich."

Then the sender went on to describe the financial chaos into which divorce had tossed her while I had been "left all that money."

What?! I'd been left money? Wow, I didn't know that. Suddenly, I was excited.

Obviously, I'm being a smart aleck. Because I know only too well I wasn't left a windfall. In fact, my husband couldn't be bothered with basic savings programs. Yes, finances were a major source of our arguments because of our differing backgrounds. In college, he had his own checking account, which his parents replenished upon request. I, on the other hands, had been raised in a family that said you had to save money for a rainy day, even at great sacrifice.

Once I told him, "We've got to start saving. I don't want to wind up as a bag lady."

He laughed. "You just don't get it, do you? I don't want anything to happen to my dad, but someday we're going to be left an enormous inheritance. We don't have to worry about a thing."

Inadvertently, I shivered, perhaps with a premonition.

"I don't know what's going to happen," I replied. "But that's not how it's going to be."

And, unfortunately, I was right. When my husband died, I was tossed into financial rough waters—just like every other single mother. Yes, I did get a small settlement from his school district, but it didn't come close to what his salary would have been.

But why had the writer of that letter to Dr. Dobson resented me? Because she *assumed* the truth. And in her own pain, she thought the rest of world was better off. No, it wasn't money that kept my children and me off the streets but my own hard-earned education. My first paying job was at 13, when a retirement home needed kitchen help and was willing to overlook my age. Throughout high school and college, I worked as a janitor, waitress, summer sports director, secretary, babysitter, salad girl—to name just a few jobs. Checks were saved for college. Stray coins on the sidewalk were instant treasure.

So if you want to resent me, pick other reasons. Resent me for working my way through college when my friends were dropping out to buy nice cars and hike through Europe. Resent me for not having to go to court to ask permission to move out of state. Resent me for not having to share my children at holidays with an ex-husband and his new family. But please don't resent me because of an imaginary insurance check.

Obviously, I hope you won't resent me at all. After all, our challenges as single mothers are intense no matter how we arrived at this station. And we need the encouragement and strength other veteran single mothers can offer.

Where's My Faith? You Ask

Some folks will be upset over my including this chapter in the book, saying if my faith were sound, I wouldn't worry about paying bills. But it's always amazed me that the people who admonish single mothers not to worry about money are the very ones who don't have to worry themselves!

My faith is intact, thank you, and I truly do believe God provides for His children. However, I'm also a believer in the old saying, "God gives every bird its food, but He doesn't throw it into the nest!"

Other folks like to remind me that money is evil. Wrong. First Timothy 6:10 says, "The *love* of money"—not money itself— "is the root of all evil" (*KJV*, emphasis added.)

Jesus paid for our sins on the Cross (see Phil. 2:5-8; Col. 1:20), but it's up to us to pay our bills. And because the Lord understands we have bills to pay, He wants us to talk over our finances with Him.

Pay God First

One area we need to take care of first is the tithe. Even though the tithe is based on Old Testament practice rather than New Testament command, I'm convinced supporting God's work is

one of our responsibilities. For years, I've helped three missionary families in addition to giving to our local church.

Some pastors teach we are to support our church first
with the full tithe and then support missionaries with gifts
beyond the tithe. I remember, for instance, a Detroit pastor
who said, "Support where you worship. After all, you don't
dine at one restaurant and then go next door and pay the bill
at another."

Good point. But talk over your giving with the Lord, and ask
Him what He wants you to do with your tithe. If you're convinced you can't give a full monetary tithe right now, consider
tithing your time or talent by teaching a Sunday School class or
painting a mural for the nursery. The important thing is to give
back to the Lord a portion of what He has given you.

A caution here though: However we decide to pay our tithe, we
should do so out of a spirit of thankfulness rather than expecting
God to pay us back "10 times over" or "a hundredfold"—as some
preachers insist. We can never outgive God, of course, but neither
does He *owe* us anything.

What We Need to Be

Be Resolute

Make rules and keep them. A January 1 radio program of the late
Christian financial advisor Larry Burkett offered four major reso-
lutions we can readily adopt to help us with our financial juggling.

- Use no credit cards.
- Reduce existing debt.
- Balance your checkbook each month to the penny.
- Determine to conquer your biggest personal financial
  problem—whether it's overspending or impulse-buying.[1]

To that list, I would add only these.

- Pray about every expense and allow the Lord to show you creative ways to solve financial problems.
- Discard envy of everyone you think has an easier time. I know several married couples who are struggling to pay their bills, too.

Say no a lot. Don't we wish we had a dollar for every time we've heard our kids say, "But I *need* a new pair of jeans!"?

I loved buying clothes for my kids, so this was an area in which I really had to get tough with myself. One thing that helped me was to involve both teens in my check-writing sessions. In amazement, they'd watch the deposit decrease steadily as I wrote checks for the house payment, utilities, groceries, car maintenance and numerous piddling expenses.

Another friend decided on a more dramatic visual aid. She cashed her check into dollar bills, which she then stacked in the middle of the table. She allowed her children to handle the dollars and exclaim, "Wow, we're rich!" Then she began to pay bills, asking each child to take turns counting out the amount needed. Finally, they were down to nine dollars but still had three bills on the table. "What shall we do now?" she asked. She had made her point and didn't have to use the visual aid again.

We single mothers can help our children set realistic limits by refusing to give in on the clothing allowance. It's amazing how our teens don't need quite so many clothes when they have to pay for all items past that set amount.

Some of my friends solve the problem by giving the entire budgeted clothing amount to the teen on each birthday and announcing it has to last the entire year. But that won't work if you can't stand to watch your youngster spend the entire amount on a "perfect" outfit early in the year and then wear worn clothing those last couple of months before the new budget kicks in.

I didn't have the money to give my kiddos their clothing allowance all at once. But even if I had, I probably would have caved later if they had started looking pitiful. Thus, what worked for me was to set an amount to spend on each teen for the year and then just say no a lot.

Think others, not things. When we were in New York and getting bogged down again in longing for *things*, I'd pull rank (mothers *are* allowed to do that) and plan a day trip to New York City.

We'd catch the Saturday morning 10:03 A.M. train out of the Chappaqua station and ride for a spellbinding 55 minutes south. Jay and I marveled at the people representing all social levels at Grand Central Station, from the Wall Street broker types to the folks panhandling for spare change. But Holly felt as though I'd sentenced her to an unbearable day of dirt and noise. In the evening, when the three of us arrived home, it was always with a new appreciation for our clean, comfortable home.

One early December Saturday, a fur-coated matron got on the train with us at Chappaqua and chirped for 45 minutes to her preteen daughter about their planned Christmas shopping at several expensive shops.

As our train pulled into the 125th Street station—located in the heart of one of New York City's most tired areas—the woman looked out the window at the decrepit apartment buildings and exclaimed, "Ugh! Why don't they move out of here?"

Holly turned to me, stunned at the woman's insensitivity to economic conditions. I nodded my head ever so slightly in acknowledgment, but the woman had made my point about materialism far better than I ever could have.

And live within your means. When we were a two-salaried family, we made purchases that were ridiculously unnecessary. As a single mother, I never had to worry about that since we were forced to live within our means.

To help keep my budget in line, I have always refused to pay for adventures with a credit card. Even a little bit of debt can start us on a spiraling descent into financial disaster. Besides, debt is one sure way to have less than nothing!

We live in a society that equates money with success and blessing, so we American Christians often have a special problem in this area, especially since we want our children to fit in and have everything we didn't. But, remember, God promised to supply our *needs*—not our *wants*—so set aside the thought that if we're faithful to Him, He's going to give us everything we want. To insist that He will denies the faith of countless Christians within the inner city, in my beloved Kentucky mountains and in Third World countries.

Be Courageous

You may occasionally have to use a little good ol' gumption, too.

When my Ethiopian friend, Marta, and her family arrived in the United States after escaping from the Marxists who had taken over her country, she was convinced a house would help them rebuild their lives. But they had arrived in the States as refugees; she didn't have money for the down payment. After much time in prayer, she visited the local bank president. He impatiently asked her to state her case quickly.

Marta described the house she wanted, confessed she didn't have any money but emphasized her hard work. And then she ran her fingers along the edge of his desk.

"I am here. I can fall this way," she said, and—to underscore her point—she gestured toward the solid desktop. "Or I can fall this way," and she gestured toward the floor. "How I fall is up to you."

He stared at her for a long moment. Finally he called the loan officer into the room. "Take care of whatever this woman needs," was all he said.

Marta and her family had their home!

Be Creative

I want to remind you we don't have to have megabucks to meet our bills. Sometimes suggestions for creative ways to make extra money turn up in interesting places.

Turn trash into treasure. I once found a trash-to-treasure-type magazine article alerting me to the possibility the junky old lamp in the back of my closet was a collector's item worth $100. Before I read the article, I'd planned to sell the old relic at our annual garage sale—probably with a $2 price tag!

Set aside now for small needs later. In addition to the universal junk drawer, I have two special drawers that get me past little financial problems: the change drawer and the gift drawer.

It seemed as though Jay and Holly always needed a dollar for something at school, so every few days I would toss loose change and an occasional spare bill into a small drawer. More than once, in addition to the school field-trip fees, the drawer's yield provided enough quarters for half a tank of gasoline or even an impromptu trip to our favorite ice-cream shop.

The contents of the second drawer—the gift drawer—have gotten me through more than one situation in which I've needed a last-minute gift. Each time I find a bargain table containing such items as an Amish cookbook or pretty stationery, I buy them at the reduced prices and stash them away to await "emergencies."

Try a do-it-yourself Christmas. Holidays can throw another heavy ball into the mix that a single mom is already juggling. During the approach of one particular Christmas, I found myself asking, *How are we going to handle presents?*

I learned long ago that the greatest gift we can give our children is a pleasant memory. Jay and Holly don't remember the expensive toys and intense decorating that were part of their earlier holidays—when we'd been a two-salaried family—but they do remember our first December as a family of three: We impulsively donned snow suits over our pajamas one midnight to make snow angels on the front lawn.

I thought of the coupon books they had made when they were in elementary school. I still have the one Holly made for me when she was 7. In large, wobbly printing, she promised to help me with grocery shopping and dust the low parts of the tables. Maybe I'll redeem those coupons when I'm 90.

For our first Colorado Christmas, the move had drained the family resources, so it was time to go back to creative gifts. The four adults and 10 children of the Lost and Found Gang were coming for Christmas Dinner, but we were going to have to rethink gift giving. So three weeks before Christmas, and over one of my inexpensive pasta dinners, the adults and I agreed the only gifts we'd exchange would be acts of service or items we'd made.

Christmas was incredible! Our family part of the day started with our own early morning gift exchange in which Jay gave Holly tickets for math help, and Holly promised to do several loads of his wash. One of Jay's gifts to me was a sheet of coupons for eight long walks—a sacrifice for my nonwalker! One of Holly's gifts was a free verse poem entitled "Parenting," in which she thanked me for being "a great person and mom."

Of course I cried when I read it. After all, many parents don't have things like that said about them until they're dead! Not having any money forced the kids to come up with creative solutions and ideas that I hope they'll share with their own children someday.

A few hours later, our guests arrived for dinner, each bringing a special dish to create a bountiful table. When it was time to open gifts, we exchanged plates of cookies, promises for help with errands and delightful homemade gifts—such as avocado candlesticks. It was an incredible day—and all because we were determined not to let a lack of money spoil our fun.

Be Wise

My heart goes out to the young mothers who need to find a reputable, reasonably priced lawyer to handle the mountain of details involved in any divorce. Ask at your church for recommendations. Call your local chamber of commerce for a list of legal offices offering *pro bono* (free) services. Just do not wring your hands and feel overwhelmed.

Some folks struggle with whether the whole process is biblical. If you're hesitant about seeking legal counsel, please remember God Himself mandated government and has said we are subject to its laws and practices. Also, if you are afraid for your safety, don't hesitate to call the police for a restraining order. Your safety—and that of your children—is paramount.

Overwhelmingly across the country, fathers aren't paying the child support they promised. Many, if they can get away with it, avoid support payments altogether. Others who pay grudgingly—and would rather not pay at all—work harder at getting their payments reduced than in meeting their rightful obligations.

Just recently, for instance, my friend Allison received an official notice that her ex had applied for a reduction *by half* of his support payments. Allison's financial struggles have certainly put my own grief into perspective. At least I don't have to hear ugly comments from an ex-husband about his "pouring money down a rat hole" to support the children he fathered. Nor do I need to cringe when the mailman delivers another letter from the Friend of the Court.

And Be Realistic

Much as we may not like it, we have to be realistic and recognize that—contrary to our rosy expectations, beautiful dreams and lovely fantasies—life isn't always fair.

Statistics report that after a divorce, the single mom's income is cut at least in half. And therein lies the divorced mom's greatest envy—if her husband had died, she wouldn't have the hassle of an ex, plus maybe she'd at least have some money.

But as I've stated, widows don't necessarily inherit lots of money. Too, my husband's dad changed his will to leave the bulk of his estate to his two surviving sons, telling them, "This family has always left the money to the children, not to the grandchildren. Whatever Jay and Holly need, their mother will make sure they get it."

I suppose I should have accepted his comment as a compliment, but it hurt to think my children were being bypassed because I'm a hard worker. And, at first, I griped to the Lord about this injustice.

Then one sunny afternoon as I waited in the school parking lot to pick up Jay and Holly, I read Hebrews 6:10. "God is not unjust; he will not forget your work and the love you have shown him as you have helped his people and continue to help them."

The words were so exactly what I needed that if an angel had tapped on the car window and given me a thumbs-up sign, I wouldn't have been surprised. I've thought of that assurance numerous times since, especially when those "it's not fair" feelings surface again. And God has not forgotten you and your children, either.

Try Thinking Double

Consider Double Duty
Several married friends are working second jobs—often menial—to keep from losing their house in the face of company closings.

And they count out nickels and dimes from the kitchen change jar to buy gasoline—just as we single moms do.

It's almost a given for single mothers to have a second job. Allison works a double nursing shift on those weekends when her ex-husband has the children. Laura bakes and decorates cakes after long days as a cashier. Chris, an elementary school teacher, gives piano lessons in the evening.

Consider Doubling Up

Some single moms have to make even greater adjustments: cutting living expenses by renting an apartment with another single mom. Ecclesiastes 4:9-10 supports that idea: "Two are better than one, because they have a good return for their work: If one falls down, his friend can help him up. But pity the man who falls and has no one to help him up!"

Of course, it can be tricky to find a landlord who will rent to two moms and their children. But I know two sisters in Michigan—with five children between them—who prayed, knocked on several doors and finally convinced an owner to rent to them on a trial basis. For the past five years, they've maintained the home so well the owner has made other rentals available to single mothers.

One caution, though: No perfect relationships exist here on Earth, so talk everything through with the other party before you enter into such an arrangement.

Don't assume anything!

Save Now for Your Retirement

Magazine articles and financial books give us hearty advice about investments, but most of us can't follow those tips because we're scrambling to buy groceries. We keep hoping we can save money "next year," but next year never seems to come along. Meanwhile, we find ourselves getting farther and farther down the road to retirement age.

If your situation is like mine, you don't have the funds to make investments right now. But hear me. You must put something away for your retirement—even if it's only a dollar a week—in an account you never touch.

I realize most banks require a minimum balance of a couple hundred dollars. But if you talk to an official, the rule can be bent for accounts that won't have withdrawals. Besides, something about seeing an account swell encourages us to save even more.

And check out the retirement plan at your work. For many of us that's the easiest way to save since the money is taken out before we see it.

You might also consider an evening surfing the Internet to explore saving and investment ideas. But I don't recommend setting up online accounts without talking to someone at your local bank or at your tax preparer's office.

If you don't have access to the Internet on your home computer, your library can help. My local library allows us to use the computers for an hour a day—free. You can also scan books and magazines in the financial section while your kids browse for books. Before I was forced to figure out ways to pay my bills and plan for that not-so-distant retirement, I'd never realized our local library subscribed to every financial magazine and shelved dozens of the latest books on putting together a budget. Undoubtedly, yours does, too.

If you're like me, you're thinking, *I don't have time to read the paper. How on Earth am I going to have time to read a financial magazine or surf the Web—or even think about a budget? And my two-year-old would never quietly "browse."*

Well, if your children are younger, and you don't have home access to the Web, you may want to trade babysitting services for one quiet evening a month. In any case, this is one ball we dare not drop.

Inventory Everything

Household Inventory

You probably possess more than you think. I realized that fact when I took a job in New York, and my insurance agent insisted I give him a household inventory. I spent several hours listing *everything* in our home—even the number of neck scarves in my dresser and a head count of the dolls in Holly's closet. When I finished, I was astonished at the items I had accumulated over the years.

Financial Inventory

That little exercise spurred me on to take a financial inventory as well. A financial inventory is just a list of your assets and debits. Translated, that merely means you know the money you have coming in and the amount going out each year.

Make an actual list of your income sources and amounts, savings, investments. Then list all of your debts—including the house and car. Just putting that down on paper will give you the same sense of control it gave me.

Provide for the Possibility of Your Death

I don't like thinking about it, but single mothers die, too. Just in case the unthinkable happened, who would raise your children? Probably your ex-husband, unless other arrangements have been made. And who raises them if you're a widow? And what about your hard-earned assets? Will they belong to your kids or will your ex-husband waltz off with them?

Update Your Will

Answering questions like these makes us realize why we single mothers need an updated will to provide for our children.

As our circumstances have changed over the years, Jay and Holly have had various guardians. When we were in New York, Carl and Marilyn—dear friends from our Michigan church—consented to that responsibility.

Carl and I had taught together for 13 years, and he and Marilyn have a proven track record with their 6 children. We had planned that if I died, Jay and Holly would return to Michigan to finish high school. But once Jay turned 18, he could assume guardianship for Holly, and they could remain in Colorado. I'm grateful I have lived to see them into adulthood. But we were prepared—just in case.

List All Important Information

Keep a list of all important legal papers, addresses and other such goodies where your family can find them, if necessary. Give a copy to your lawyer, as well. Again, many law offices have provision for pro bono work.

Do you have a retirement fund? Perhaps you have an IRA or a 403(b) offered through your company. Keep all relevant information with your legal paperwork.

Remember that some companies offer survivor benefits in addition to an insurance settlement.

My few "future planning" pages begin with information needed in the event of my death or incapacity. Then I've listed close relatives' names and addresses, my lawyer's name and address, and general funeral arrangements.

I've also listed the insurance policies for my car, home and life. Next, I've listed the mortgage holder and number, as well as the account numbers for the checking and saving accounts.

I often have to fly for my job. But I don't waste energy worrying about the resulting chaos if I die—now that my will and affairs are in order.

If you are horrified by what I've just said and are thinking,

That's morbid, look at it this way: Being prepared for sudden eventualities is like owning an umbrella. You seldom need it, unless you don't plan on needing it.

Involve the Kids

Children need to be in charge of their own money, so even in their preteens, I provided Jay and Holly with a small allowance. In turn, they were expected to clear the table and load the dishwasher on alternate days, do light housecleaning and keep their own rooms neat. I accepted their differing definitions of "neat."

In addition, I kept a long list of extra jobs—sweeping out the garage, shoveling the snow, cleaning the closet—for which I'd pay extra.

And, as a balance, I charged them when they missed the school bus, and I had to taxi them to class. On some days I even warned them that my schedule was so tight that if I had to drive them to school, the price would be five dollars. Boy, you should have seen those youngsters hurry out of their rooms then!

An important part of providing on-the-job training for your kids is knowing their varying abilities. Jay would step over piles of laundry and claim he never saw them. But give him a room to paint and the job was done quickly and well, especially if he could have the radio tuned to his station.

Holly, on the other hand, never could tolerate a mess. Even when it was her turn to cook, she cleaned as she went.

Maybe your children are opposites, too. If so, you've probably already learned you'll drive yourself goofy if you expect the same results from different personalities.

Keep Good Records for the IRS

If you're highly organized, you'll want to skip this section because my annual tax preparation methods give logical minds headaches. But they work for me.

Throughout the year, I toss all my receipts into the middle bureau drawer. Then long about January 1, I start worrying about sorting them into several piles—missions and charity receipts, freelance writing income and expenses, mortgage interest, professional expenses and so on.

When I'm tired of dreading the chore, I finally declare a particular evening to be "tax night" and sort everything into stacks. When they lived at home, Jay and Holly would anticipate the arrival of tax night and tried to have something else planned.

Then, once everything is organized, it takes another evening to total all the numbers and get them ready for my tax preparer. If you are more organized than my "piling system," you may want to invest in Quick Books or Excel software. Whatever you choose, though, remind yourself of all you have conquered already. This is just one more hurdle you *can* sail over.

Remember, God Works in Mysterious Ways

Even with carefully thought-out plans and much prayer, life's circumstances don't always go the way we want them to.

Crisis

Shortly after we settled into Colorado, I learned that the buyer for our New York condo—overlooking a parking lot—had listed the assets she *hoped* to have by the time of closing rather than what she actually had. As a result, the deal fell through.

Suddenly, I was the not-so-proud owner of two mortgages. Meanwhile, the struggling economy caused the East Coast market to fall. My first job at 13 had taught me the penny-by-penny value of a dollar, so I was terrified at the amount I would lose if

I were forced to forfeit the down payment I had paid on the condo.

Questions

The turn of events catapulted me into almost two months of rereading the Scriptures I felt had led me to move West. I fought the fear that I'd somehow missed God's direction and often had to shake myself mentally and remind myself that my motivation for the rapid move was to get Jay and Holly settled in Colorado before their first day of school.

The more I read the Word, the more I was reassured that God had opened the doors for the move. I was also reminded of two things: God has promised His children trouble (see John 16:33), and He will always be with them in the trouble (again, see John 16:33).

I'd made my decision based on the information I'd had at the time, and no amount of hindsight was going to change the way things had turned out. All I could do now was give the situation to the Lord, trust Him to bring His good out of it and stop listening to so-called friends who said maybe I wasn't supposed to have moved since the New York sale had fallen through. (Why do people do that to us?)

Surrender

I fretted and prayed for weeks. Then I reached the end of my emotional rope: One morning on my before-work walk, I said aloud to the Lord, "Okay, I'm done with it. Do what You want."

Wouldn't it be wonderful to report He sold my place that very afternoon? Believe me, I wish it had happened. But, instead, my declaration forced me to stop begging for an immediate sale and to name those things for which I could be thankful. And so I began to pray:

Thank You, Father, for this new job.
Thank You for this incredible sky.
Thank You for the sight of snow-covered Pikes Peak.
Thank You for the good health allowing
me to take this walk.
Thank You Jay's not on drugs.
Thank You Holly's not pregnant.

The next morning I randomly thumbed through my Bible, not sure what I was looking for. Suddenly I stopped at Judges 20—the account of the Israelites asking the Lord if they were to fight the Benjamites. Twice He told them to fight. And twice they were soundly defeated—having lost 22,000 men the first day and 18,000 men the second day (see Judg. 20:21-25)!

Trust
It wasn't until the third battle that He gave victory to the Israelites. Why had God wasted 40,000 men (see Judg. 20:33-36)? At least in the Book of Job, the reader knows that Job, a righteous man, suffered because of a conversation between Satan and God. But I found no such clue in the Judges 20 account. I was back to having to walk by blind faith that God *was* working even if I couldn't see the results.

That afternoon, a Monday, I pulled the last of my savings out to pay the bills—including both mortgages—bought groceries and thanked the Lord we still had $34 to get us through the next month. I was feeling calm. We could coast for 4 weeks.

Complications
Then Jay came home from school. "Oh, Mom, don't forget I have to pay for my chamber choir tux by this Wednesday. And I can't be in the choir without it."

I held my breath. "How much?"

"Seventy dollars." He was digging into a box of cheese snacks. The kitchen chair squeaked as I sat down. "Well, Jay, this is going to be interesting to see how the Lord works this out."

Holly strolled in then, so I had them both sit with me.

I opened the checkbook, explained the situation and said, "You know the prayer that went into our move. But if I've somehow missed the Lord's voice, then we're going to face some rough times ahead until He chooses to take us through the problem. And if I haven't missed His voice then I guess He's just trying to teach me something."

Both kiddos stared at the checkbook for a long time.

Jay spoke first. "No, I think God's trying to teach Holly and me to depend on Him instead of on good ol' Mom."

I pondered that. Then said, "Maybe. But either way, we're starting an adventure. We're going to see God work in ways that never would have been possible without this mess. And you may discover the joys of soup beans and cornbread, but God won't let us go hungry. My Kentucky days are going to pay off!"

Jay shook his head at the mention of the beans. "That's carrying a good attitude too far, Mom."

I leaned forward as I said, "And I'm telling you we're going to be all right. You just watch what the Lord is going to do. If He chooses not to sell that goofy place, then He'll help us meet the payments somehow."

Prayer

I continued. "Remember the story of how England's George Müeller and the orphans he cared for sat at an *empty* table and thanked God for the food they were about to receive? And before they finished their prayer, a baker was at the door, saying he'd baked too many loaves of bread that morning, and could they use them? And what about when the milk wagon had broken down, and the driver didn't want to take the milk back to the dairy?

"Well, you just wait and see how the Lord takes care of your need for that $70."

Then we prayed, thanking the Lord for His future provision.

Provision

The next day's mail brought an unexpected utility bill—and a rebate check from Allied Van Lines for $254!

Right now you may be thinking, *So you didn't have money to cover the purchase of a tux. Big deal. We should all have such small problems.*

True, whether or not we bought the school tuxedo was hardly a life-and-death matter. But as a mother, I recognized that having the tux made possible something of real importance to my son, and that fact made it important to me.

As a child of God, I truly believe that what is important to one of His children is also important to Him. And He demonstrated such truth by intervening and meeting a particular need which—though of no great consequence in itself—was a matter of real importance to a mother and son seeking His help.

In the following weeks, we watched pennies like never before—and continued to tithe. Gradually, every bill was taken care of, and the condo eventually sold. Yes, at less than what I paid for it, but at least I was free of that staggering financial responsibility.

A New Understanding

That scary time certainly gave me a new understanding of the financial crises here in Colorado—and across the nation during our recession.

I started a Bible study group for professional women every Thursday. One woman asked for prayer, remarking that her husband's business had failed and her temporary job was the only thing allowing them to keep their home. In the past, of course I would have prayed, but now my own experience gave greater depth to my petitions on her behalf.

I've also discovered joy in being stone-cold broke: No one bothered calling me with a sad story and a request for a loan.

A Greater Good

The Lord always brings His good out of our problems—if we'll let Him. And He'll always provide for us, but sometimes we have to get a little creative.

If my brakes had gone out on the car while we had only the $34, I would have been in trouble since I'm too stubborn to ask even the church for help. I would have been more prone to barter services—offer to clean the repair office for several weeks or even provide child care for the mechanic's baby.

Chris, a single mother in our Sunday School class, told us about the unexpected bill for $117 marked "pay upon receipt." Her paycheck wasn't due until the end of the month, but instead of panicking, she gathered her three children for prayer and brainstorming. Her oldest daughter, 12, came up with the idea of a garage sale that coming weekend. With no time or money to put an ad in the paper, they prayed again—and then cleaned out closets and the garage for items they no longer used. Chris described the numerous cars that stopped at the sale, then dramatically asked, "Guess how much money we made that day?" Exactly $117. What an answer to prayer! And what a faith-building lesson for her—and for her children.

Occasionally, I'm asked if I'd go on welfare if I had to do so. The phrase "had to" is tough to define, so I usually mutter that I trust the Lord to keep meeting our needs. But if a single mom is desperate, and no help is available except welfare, then, by all means, I want her to keep feeding her children.

A Deeper Faith

My concern is for those who look first to the government for help instead of to the Lord. I've also seen what the welfare system has done to my beloved Kentucky, robbing many of the people of that wonderful, tough mountain ingenuity.

So let's try, as single moms, to be a little more faith-filled and creative than the rest of the world.

Once More with Feeling

- Money itself isn't evil. First Timothy 6:10 says, "The *love* of money is the root of all evil" (*KJV*, emphasis added). The Lord understands we have bills to pay, and He wants us to talk over our finances with Him.
- The tithe is not an obligation but a privilege allowing us to have a part in God's work. We are to give as He prospers us, so remember to pay God first.
- Apply these four suggestions for gaining financial control: Use no credit cards, reduce existing debt, balance your checkbook each month, and determine to conquer your biggest personal financial problem.
- Pray about every expense and allow the Lord to show you creative ways to solve your problem.
- Be both courageous and creative as you look for ways to stretch your budget.
- Dwell on Hebrews 6:10 rather than life's unfairness: "God is not unjust; he will not forget your work and the love you have shown him as you have helped his people and continue to help them."
- Retirement planning isn't an *option* for us, but a *must*.
- Don't be intimidated by words such as "budget" and

"financial inventory." Those are ways to gain control over your financial life.

· Making a will and choosing guardians for your children are safeguards for your children's future.

· Children need to be in charge of a small amount of money. An allowance and opportunities to make extra money teach important lessons.

· Keep good records for the IRS.

· Though He may work in mysterious ways, God is always in control.

Note

1. Larry Burkett, radio broadcast, January 1, 1991.

Any Houseboats for Sale or Rent?

Suppose one of you wants to build a tower. Will [you] not first sit down and estimate the cost to see if [you have] enough money to complete it?

LUKE 14:28

I'm one of those who never gets on a plane without knowing where the emergency doors are. And when I check into a hotel, I locate my floor's exit. Once I've determined my way of escape, then I go about my normal, cheerful business.

Jay and Holly have watched me do that for years, so when we were en route to visit relatives a while back, they insisted I stop thinking the worst. I assured them I was merely being prepared "just in case." But I gave in to their insistence, and that night in our hotel I didn't look for the stairs nearest our room.

You know what happened next, of course. Yep, early the next morning, the fire bell went off. For a startled moment, we looked at one another, not believing what we were hearing.

But I was the adult, so with seeming calmness I announced, "It's okay. Let's just get out of here."

I felt the door—no heat—and then opened it, and we stepped out into a pitch black hallway. Not even the usual exit-sign lights were visible.

"O Lord, help us," I implored.

Immediately, we heard a woman speaking with a heavy Spanish accent. "Is anyone on this floor?" she asked.

"Three of us," I answered.

"Come this way," she said. "Follow my voice."

With Jay and Holly hanging on to my arms, I felt along the wall as we moved toward the woman. At last we could see her in her maid's uniform, standing near the fire door.

I thanked her, but she waved toward the door. "It's okay. But do hurry."

The fire was quickly contained, and we were able to return to our rooms to claim our luggage for checkout.

Amazingly, we didn't see that particular maid with the rest of the staff in the parking lot. Isn't it interesting she appeared as soon as I asked the Lord for help? To this day, we wonder if perhaps heaven had responded by sending an angel to guide us.

We don't always receive such direct, on-the-spot answers to our petitions, of course. But every now and again, I'm convinced, God *does* intervene directly—or via His messengers. So keep watching. You never know what form the miraculous will take.

Oh, by the way, Jay and Holly have never again teased me about being prepared "just in case."

Be Prepared

Being prepared is just a part of my nature now. That approach to life and the fact I don't like surprises—even happy surprises—caused me to put a lot of preparation and energy into making sure any major purchase I made was right for me and my family.

As a single mom, I have found that the two biggest headaches have been what to drive and where to live. And since I suspect these are probably problem areas for you, too, let's take a look at what is involved in buying a car and buying or renting a house, as the Lord and the budget permit.

Know What to Look for When Buying a Used Car

And why should you consider buying a used car? Because it costs less than a new one.

Yet, we've all heard it said that when you buy a used car you may be buying someone else's problems. Yes, that's why your reputable mechanic is going to be invaluable to you if you don't have a trusted friend to help you pick out a car.

So remember this rule: *Before you buy a used car, make sure the seller will agree to your having it checked out by your own mechanic.* That checkup may cost you a few dollars, but it will be worth it in the long run.

Where to Start

If you don't have a predetermined car manufacturer in mind and don't have the foggiest notion where to begin, just keep calm and do your homework. Sure, that's work, but we're used to hard work. After all, we're single moms!

Here are some tips.

Check out the Consumer Reports *website or take a trip to the library some evening and thumb through* Consumer Reports *to see which cars have the best safety and maintenance records.*

If your kids are old enough, take them along with you to the library, and let them select their cache of books to take home. Reading opens new worlds for all of us, so I hope you are encouraging that area.

If you choose the library, and your youngsters are too little to enjoy it, get a friend to stay with them or hire a sitter for the evening. Even if a sitter's fee strains the budget a bit at the time, you'll find the money well invested because of what you'll eventually save with your newly acquired smarts when you make a wise car buy later.

Call your insurance agent for his recommendation on a car. Your insurance can vary considerably with year, make and model, so you need to consider the cost of insurance protection before you start looking.

Start looking for a car within your own social group. It's a good place to start, as a friend will usually tell you if something is wrong with a car he or she is hoping to sell you. Don't forget to check the bulletin boards at work, too.

Know how much you can afford to pay. And once you've set that figure, don't allow yourself to be talked into spending "just a little bit more." Those multiplied "little bits" are what keep us all enslaved to debt.

Financial advisors say if we can't afford to save for a major purchase, then we can't afford the purchase. But while I agree with that statement in principle, I also know the reality of needing a car and not having the savings to cover it.

Know what to ask. After Jay and Holly both had their drivers' licenses, they decided to pool their savings and share a used car. They studied the classifieds for days and then began making calls. They even had a list of questions.

1. What's the general condition?
2. May I have my mechanic check it over?
3. Can the car pass the emissions test? That's an important question in our state because if it can't, we can't get license plates for it.

4. Would you recommend this as my first car? I've been pleased by the sellers who've warned them not to buy their car since that particular model had a lot of problems.

It took a while for my teens to agree on a car they could afford, but when they found it, all their work caused them to appreciate it all the more.

How to Proceed

After you've done your research, you can start visiting the car lots. Many magazine articles suggest you take a male friend along, but that's impossible for those of us who have moved away from our friends. As a rule, I've found most salesmen want to be helpful, so don't assume every used car salesman is out to cheat you.

If the salesman is rude—as one was to me with his "Tell you what, honey, why don't you have your husband come in and talk to me?"—politely tell him you're taking your business someplace else because of his rudeness and then leave. But scenes like that are rare, so don't walk in with a chip on your shoulder.

Whatever else you do, just don't buy the first thing you look at—if for no other reason than to satisfy your own future questions about what else might have been available. And, as you visit the various car lots, do carry a notebook to jot down important details: size of car, whether it's a four- or six-cylinder engine (the number of cylinders merely determines the power you'll have on the expressway), the general condition, the mileage and the price.

Next, ask to see the "blue book" price on that car. If you belong to a credit union, give them a quick phone call and they'll be happy to supply that information. The "blue book" is published by the National Automobile Dealers Association and is properly called the *NADA Official Used Car Guide*.

It lists the average trade-in value, the retail price and the amount of credit you can expect to receive for it. But remember their listing is made up of averages. How much you pay for your particular car will depend on the car's condition, supply-and-demand, the locale and the trade-in value of your present car—if you have one.

What to Look for

All I'd ever seen anyone do in movies was kick the tires—a sure sign of an amateur. So, when my car's engine went out, I talked to anybody who was interested in cars, asked questions and read several magazine articles. From all that, I developed a mental list of what I needed in a car: four doors, a big trunk and enough engine power to keep me safe on our Detroit expressway.

Here are some things I learned:

Check the car's exterior. Look for dents, rust, discolored paint and welding ripples. Metal ripples or uneven paint are clues that the car has been in an accident. That's especially important if the frame has been bent. And deep rust means the car is rusting from the inside out. That problem could mean a major repair will be due soon.

Check the interior. Examine the controls—wipers, heat and air, turn signals, radio and all lights. And look under the mats and loose carpet for rust. Also look at the odometer to check the mileage. Then look at the gas pedal. If the pedal's well worn, but the odometer shows low mileage, that's a pretty good sign they've rolled back the mileage. Also, if the numbers don't line up evenly, someone has been messing with the odometer.

Look under the hood. This is the scary part for me. Are the belts and hoses worn? Does the radiator show corrosion or rust around the cap? Is the battery corroded? Does it have worn cables?

Start the engine. As the car idles, accelerate and listen for pings or knocks. That's a sign of potential engine problems. My neighbor Keith talked about "valves" and "rings" in the same sentence as "knocks," but it all translated into "engine problems." Keith also said to let the car run for five minutes and then check under it for puddles. If they're greasy, you could have transmission problems.

Take the car for a drive. It's called a "test drive," because you're supposed to be *testing* the brakes, steering and general handling.

Trust your instincts. Listen for unusual noises when you shift, accelerate or brake. Don't ignore any pulling or jerking.

See? It's not so scary when we know what we're looking for.

Know What to Do When Looking for a New Car

If, after looking at all the used cars available in your area, you decide you want a new car after all and you plan to drive it forever—I've put more than 175,000 miles on my car in just a few years—you need to be aware of a few things.

Don't Splurge

Car dealers aren't in business for their health, so they're going to try to tack everything on to that new car they can—tilt steering wheel, cruise control, automatic windows and so on. These are all nice conveniences but certainly not worth the cost for someone who's having to watch dollars—pennies! So just stay with the essentials.

Do Negotiate

You aren't buying a loaf of bread with a fixed price. You're trying to get your best price on something that can be purchased for less than the sticker price. So go for it.

Ask Lots of Questions

And don't be timid about asking for sufficient information on those expensive "extras." When I bought my first car, the young salesman tried to sell me a fabric-protector package for several hundred dollars.

I leaned forward and quietly asked, "What does it *actually* do?"

He gave me an elaborate song-and-dance about the importance of protecting the car's interior from spills.

I gave him the look I normally used on students who thought they were putting one over on "Ol' Lady Aldrich" and asked the question again. "But what does it actually do?"

He blushed, then stammered, "For four bucks, buy a can of fabric protector and spray the seats."

I did exactly that.

Continue to Be Prepared*After* You Buy Your Car

How would you handle one of Colorado's sudden spring storms that can dump up to a foot of snow within a few hours? Even the threat of such an ordeal made me pack an emergency kit in the trunk.

In it I have a bag of cat litter for traction in case I get stuck in an icy parking lot, a first-aid kit, a flashlight and flashers, jumper cables, road maps, simple tools, a can of instant flat-fixer, ice scrapers, a folding shovel and a pair of old boots.

The National Weather Service says I should also have a blanket or a sleeping bag, foil-wrapped matches, candles, paper towels, an extra coat, socks and gloves, nonperishable food such as peanut butter and raisins, a compass, and a pocket knife.

That's next week's car project.

Learn How to Do Simple Auto Maintenance

When I was part of a traditional family, my world was divided into neat little categories labeled "his job" and "my job." Taking care of the cars was definitely on the husband side of things, so I never thought about needing transmission fluid or even changing the oil every 3,000 miles. But I'd learned early if I tackled a new chore, it quickly became my job. And like a lot of things in life, since I had never attempted it, I was afraid of it.

Maintain fluid levels. One afternoon, I had just straightened up from putting the latest license plates on the car when our neighbor Bill pulled into his driveway. Seeing the pliers in my hand, he strolled over to see if I needed help. When I proudly explained what I had just accomplished, he nodded.

"That's great," he teased, "But I won't be impressed until I come home and see you working *under* the car."

I had my challenge. That evening, I invited my other special neighbors, Keith and Betty, over for coffee and forewarned them I was going to ask how to maintain my car.

Keith's a natural teacher, so we stood in my driveway with the hood of my car open to a mysterious view of The Engine. And that night I had my first lesson in maintaining my old blue car: keeping the levels up of the transmission fluid and power steering fluid.

Change the oil. The next night, Keith changed my oil while I took notes. The instructions about changing the oil filter include a quotation from Keith: "Don't rush—make sure you have all afternoon." Next to that statement, I've written a note to myself: "Make sure *Keith* is home."

The first time I changed the oil by myself, not only did I make sure Keith was home, but I also timed it so that Bill—the neighbor who had handed me the original challenge—would be pulling into his driveway while I was under my car. He was duly impressed.

That little scene took place before the arrival of the 10-minute oil change pits on every corner. Now I take my car to them and pay the few dollars every 3,000 miles. But I'm still proud I *can* change my own oil if I want to or need to.

Avoid panic. The more you understand about your car, the less afraid of it you'll be and the less likely it is that you'll be taken in by a not-so-honest mechanic. A good place to start learning is by reading the owner's manual that comes with the car—if you haven't already tossed it or lost it. I finally got around to reading the one that had been lying untouched in the glove compartment of my own car since day one.

Also, many community colleges offer basic maintenance courses. It's worth a couple evenings of your time to learn about your car, so you'll no longer fear it.

Find a reputable repair shop. The best thing you can do to keep your car running smoothly for a long time is to have it maintained regularly. So ask your friends for recommendations of reputable repairmen. I depend on the service department of my local dealership.

Where to Live

If you think I've agonized over the car, you should have seen me trying to decide where to live!

I realize today's young women know far more about leasing apartments and buying houses on their own than I did. But if you share some of my earlier concerns, remember the most important first step is prayer. But even with prayer, you still may have plenty of work to do.

When we were planning to move to Colorado, I had only two afternoons to look for housing. But I'd been praying for a couple of weeks, so I knew the type of house we needed. I called the realtor who's since become my friend, and I detailed both the house

I wanted and the school district I wanted it in. She arranged for me to see 23 houses.

The house I purchased was the second place I looked at. As soon as I walked in, I *knew* it was my house. But I didn't say anything and let the realtor show me all the other houses on her list. She teased me later about going through all that, but we both knew I had to see what was on the market.

When You're Looking to Buy

Since I've purchased different homes in different places at different times without even a good friend accompanying me, I want to pass along some of the things I've learned.

Do your homework first. Talk to school administrators, pastors and anyone else who will answer your questions. We were still living in New York when I started narrowing our choices for a school district, church and neighborhood in Colorado Springs.

The only people I knew in Colorado were Ron and Sharon, dear friends and former tennis partners. Even though they lived in Boulder, about two and a half hours north of Colorado Springs, I wasn't bashful about calling them.

They knew one couple in Colorado Springs and suggested I talk to them. In turn, that couple suggested I talk to two teachers, who gave me the names of several others. By the time I finished the networking calls, I had a $302 phone bill, but I also had definite direction about which school I wanted Jay and Holly to attend, which church we'd visit and which neighborhood we'd buy into.

Then start your search. Work with a realtor from a reputable firm. Not only can she answer questions about the town, but she can also give you a list of mortgage companies and make arrangements for all inspections.

Insist on a structural inspection. Face it, when we're under pressure, we have a tendency to make an emotional purchase, a kind of I-could-just see-us-living-there reaction. That's valid certainly, but an inspection will eliminate doubts and problems that *will* crop up later when we're tired and wondering if we've made the right choice.

The inspection will tell you the condition of the house and its foundation. Sure, it may cost a couple hundred dollars, but you'll know what you're buying and will sleep better at night, confident you saved yourself from an unpleasant surprise later.

If you run into a too-good-to-be-true deal, it probably is, so find out why. Some homes, for instance, can't pass a radon inspection for natural radioactive gases, so the owners are willing to sell at a ridiculous price.

Check for cracks over the inside doors. Such defects may mean the foundation has shifted.

Ask about the utility bills for the past year. If your utility bills are higher than those of your new neighbors, the house you are thinking of purchasing may have poor insulation.

Inquire about how the home is being heated. And when was the furnace last cleaned and inspected?

Notice if the driveway is cracked. Deep cracks may signal the ground is still settling. Also, our city is located over an old mining area, which occasionally experiences the collapse of underground tunnels.

Check to see if the roof is sagging. If so, you may have a serious foundation problem.

Ensure that the water pressure is adequate. To check the pressure, turn on the tap and then flush the toilet. The water flow in the tap should remain unchanged.

Don't assume anything! Ask which appliances stay with the house. Include in your offer those appliances you want to buy.

There! That's enough to get you started. The Internet, your library or local realty office will have more detailed information to help you feel more confident about your purchase. Remember, you *can* handle this, too!

When You're Looking to Rent

Okay, you've read this far and you're saying, "Sandra, come down to Earth. Right now, on my income, buying our own home is out of the question. On my pay, I'm doing well just to meet current bills and to keep groceries on the table. But we do need a decent place to live. So tell me how to find a place to rent that I can afford."

Finding decent housing when you're a single mom with children and with limited means is not easy, particularly when many landlords may not want to rent to families with small children. But, for what they're worth, here are some thoughts to get you started.

Find out what's available. You need to know who does rent to families with children—with or without pets. Talk with others in your situation. Read the classifieds closely. Make inquiries.

And look into all types of housing: single-family homes, apartments, condos, whatever. I know you're already thinking *How much?* but for the moment, don't worry if the rent for any of these places is out of your reach. Just find out if the landlords are comfortable renting to families with kids.

Now, let's assume you found something suitable, and you can swing it on your income. Great, you're all set. But what if it's going to take two incomes to swing it? Then let's look at this next suggestion.

Team up with another single mother. Have you found a nice place to live that's too expensive for one income? Or are you a divorced or widowed mother who's stuck with a house you can't afford to keep by yourself? That latter circumstance is not all bad. Since you're already in the house, at least you don't have to come up with a security deposit plus first- and last-month's rent. You just need another single mom to share ongoing costs and responsibilities.

So whether you've found something to rent that is beyond your means or are stuck with a place you can't afford to keep alone, advertise through your church, your place of work, the local supermarket bulletin board or the classifieds for another woman—ideally another single mom with kids—to share your home and expenses with you. Assuming you're compatible, you'll find sharing a home with another mom and her kids has lots of benefits.

You'll have another adult companion in the home, so you won't be forced to live entirely in the world of children. You'll have someone to share chores, as well as expenses. And if you two can keep your social life and outside commitments flexible, each of you has a resident babysitter—who works for free!—for those times when you do have to be out of the home. But make sure you talk through every detail of your expectations—and hers.

Consider mobile-home living. Check out mobile-home parks in your area. Some are adult-only or seniors-only parks. But others are designed to be family parks. And, as a rule, whether you're renting or buying, mobile homes—often called "coaches"—will cost you much less than conventional housing of comparable size.

So even though you also have to pay a monthly lot rental to the park owners, the total monthly payment for coach and lot will frequently be well below the rental of even a tiny efficiency apartment. And a single-wide coach can provide you with more bedroom space than many small apartments.

My friends who live in mobile-home parks say that, generally, a neighborly attitude prevails, benefiting all who live there. Unlike residents in apartment complexes or in conventional neighborhoods, park residents tend to look upon one another as members of an extended family more than as neighbors. They look out for one another and help each other in times of need.

Many lifelong friendships develop in mobile-home parks.

Also, many such parks offer activity programs to provide residents with a varied social life without their having to leave home. That's a real bonus for single moms: They can do something fun from time to time without running up extra babysitting bills.

Check out subsidized housing. Federally subsidized housing is available in some areas for mothers and children with limited income. Such housing is a boon for the working mother who can manage a month's rent, but cannot also come up with a security deposit and those formidable first- and last-month's rents at the same time. If you're in that situation, subsidized housing will provide you and the kids with suitable housing until they are older or until you can save enough for alternative accommodations.

Check with your nearest office of the Department of Housing and Urban Development to determine if you're eligible for their program. And even if you're eligible but have to go on a waiting list for a while because of lack of vacancies, it's still worth it to apply.

Of course, you're probably coming up with ideas of your own. I wish you well in whatever option you choose for yourself and those kiddos of yours.

By the way, don't think you are going to destroy your children if you have to "downsize" your living space for a while. Recently, I met a woman from Louisiana who told of her childhood on a bayou houseboat.

"That was the only housing my mother had been able to afford," she said. "But I never understood her embarrassment that we were living there. I loved every minute and often wish I could go back to those days."

So, yes, make sure your children are safe and surrounded by your love. But, remember, they will carry memories of that love into their adulthood, long after they have forgotten the place where you lived.

Once More with Feeling

- Always be prepared in order to avoid surprises and mechanical lemons.
- Regular maintenance will help you keep your car for a long time. And you'll save money if you learn to do the simple maintenance yourself.
- The more you understand about your car, the less frightened you'll be by it. Study your owner's manual and maybe take a course in basic maintenance.
- Know what to look for when you go to buy a used car. Then you will be less likely to be taken in by not-so-reputable salespeople and mechanics.
- Before you buy a used car, make sure the seller will agree to your having it checked by your own mechanic.
- Call your insurance agent for his recommendation before buying any car, used or new. Your insurance can vary considerably depending on the year, make and model of the car.
- Know how much you can afford. And once you've set that figure, don't let yourself be talked into spending "just a little bit more."
- If you're shopping for a house, be sure to do your homework first. Read everything you can and ask lots of questions.
- When you're buying a house, work with a realtor from a reputable firm, insist on a structural inspection and don't assume anything!

- If renting a place to live is your option, find out first all that is available to families with children.
- If suitable housing is beyond your budget, team up with another single mom and rent a place together. If the two families are compatible, the arrangement offers many benefits.
- Mobile-home living and subsidized housing are other rental possibilities worth exploring.
- Your children will carry memories of your love into their adulthood, long after they've forgotten the place where you lived.

And We're to Do All That Without Yelling?

No discipline seems pleasant at the time, but painful. Later on, however, it produces a harvest of righteousness and peace for those who have been trained by it.

HEBREWS 12:11

Early in our adjustment as a family of three, eight-year-old Holly was mean to Jay, and she even refused rudely to complete a simple household task. Her obnoxious behavior built through the morning until I finally gave her little bottom a couple of swats. She held back tears as she thrust out her lower lip, gave me one of her crushing looks and stomped upstairs.

I realize now she was testing me, but at the time I felt defeated. After a few minutes, I quietly went upstairs to see about her. She was asleep on top of her bed, her arms wrapped around her dad's picture. I felt terrible as I pulled a blanket around her tiny shoulders.

We've read enough from child experts to know that the purpose of discipline is to teach acceptable behavior today and instill self-control in the long run. We also know we're supposed to be consistent, make the rules clear and specific, criticize constructively, act promptly and issue reasonable punishment.

And we're to do all that without yelling?

Know Why You Discipline Your Children

So why do we moms struggle so? I'm convinced it's because we're often so busy with our own trauma that we merely *react* to our children, rather than thinking ahead and anticipating the problems likely to arise. Of course, helping our children develop self-discipline takes time and, since we never seem to have enough of that, all too many of us ignore the problems until they become crises.

But before we can expect our children to develop self-discipline we have to know *why* we desire it for them. One tired mother told me she'd always thought children were like little weeds—if you kept them fed and watered, they'd just naturally grow. She's since discovered it takes much more.

So what do you want for your children? Remember in *Alice in Wonderland* when Alice asked the Cheshire Cat for directions? "Where do you want to go?" he asked her.

She answered, in bewilderment, "I don't know."

"Well, then," he said, "one way is just as good as another."

Have a Discipline Road Map

List Your Goals

To help me map out my discipline route, I made an actual list of goals for my children. I wanted them to develop:

1. A close relationship with their heavenly Father
2. Spiritual discernmen
3. A balanced view of money
4. A servant's heart
5. The ability to bounce back from a mistake—but to learn from the experience

Define Your Values

Know your own values. If you aren't sure how to define those values, list all the things that are important and prioritize them. These headed my list:

God,
Jay and Holly,
work,
extended family and friends.

To help me in the constant juggling between my family and God's work, I occasionally reminded myself that if I was sacrificing my children for the sake of "God's work," it was no longer God's work.

Establish Firm Limits

Set limits and stick by them. Teens are great howlers when it comes to rules, but they gain a sense of security if they know the limits.

But remember to communicate those expectations clearly. Teens don't like hearing "Well, you should have known better" any more than we do.

Build Self-Esteem and Allow for Growth

Develop Their Self-Esteem

Work on your children's self-esteem early. If children feel good about themselves, they will resist having to prove their worth through dangerous actions or inappropriate choices of friends.

Help your children find something at which they can excel. Developing positive skills will not only bolster their self-esteem but will also result in their not having blocks of unclaimed time. The adage "Idle hands are the devil's workshop" is true.

Let Them Grow

I had so many fears about the real world "out there" that I tended to want to keep my kids under my wing. But I had grown only when I had been allowed to take responsibility, so I figured that was the only way my children were going to grow, too.

Reinforce Positive Social Development

Provide Group Experiences

Provide group experiences before the teen years. While you still have the control, get your youngster involved in the church youth group or in a community organization. Of course, it takes time to chauffeur everyone here and there, but it can pay great dividends later.

Welcome Their Friends

Welcome your child's friends. You may feel as though you're fighting a never-ending battle against the power of the peer group. But it doesn't have to be that way.

My kid's friends were always welcome in our home—especially since it allowed me to know what they were doing. Admittedly, it took time and effort to make our home available, but I know it was worth it.

Offer Your Kids Wide Shoulders to Lean On

Peer pressure can be almost overwhelming at times, and to resist such pressure may take more strength than some youngsters can muster. When that happens, your kids may break rules you and they have previously agreed upon. But these infractions are not so much acts of deliberate disobedience as they are manifestations of an inability to stand alone against one's peers and say no. At such times, our kids need our support, not our rebuke.

Be Supportive

I do remember how intense peer pressure can be, so while my own kids were in their early teens, I told them:

"When you're in a tough situation and you don't want the others to mock your decision, blame me. Just say, 'I can't. My mom would kill me. And you've seen her; you know she's capable of doing exactly that.'

"My experiences through the years have given me broad shoulders; I'm happy to carry your challenges until you're strong enough to carry them yourselves."

In those early years, I was relieved to occasionally overhear one or the other of my kiddos say into the phone, "Sorry, I can't. My mom won't let me" even though I hadn't been asked.

I'd always stroll past as though I were stone deaf. But inside I was rejoicing.

I taught high school for 15 years, so I enjoy being around teens. I loved it when Jay and Holly invited their friends over to watch a video or play a board game. I supplied the pizza, cheese and crackers, fruit and dip, and brownies. My teens knew the rules: They could invite whomever they wanted, but none of them was allowed to drink, smoke, swear or watch inappropriate movies in our home.

Admittedly, both kids invited friends who made me a little nervous, but they were still made to feel welcome. For many of them, our home was a haven, and perhaps my rules gave them an idea of what a structured family life—complete with regular dinner hours—is supposed to be.

Be Available

I didn't hang around when the youngsters had their friends over, but I always "just happened" to be baking—the results of which were served fresh out of the oven—as the friends strolled in on Friday evenings. Of course, then I was within earshot as I cleaned up the kitchen while the teens watched a movie.

Only once did we have a problem. Holly had attended the school hockey game with a group of friends. I knew the driver of her car was responsible, so I allowed her to go, and then I invited the whole gang back for pizza and a movie. I hadn't stressed they were going to watch a video I had chosen, so two of the guys brought back one from their collection.

I strolled through the family room on my way to the laundry (I always had towels to fold). Immediately, I knew this was a movie I'd rather they not watch. Still, I hesitated to shut it off, not wanting to cause a scene.

Then in the midst of my wimpy decision-making process, *the* swear word came tearing out of the screen. Not only had I heard it, but also the kids knew I'd heard it.

With the others looking out the corners of their eyes at me, I motioned for Holly to join me in the living room. Her "huh, oh" merely increased the tension.

But Be Firm

She followed me. "Well, Holly, you know the video is going to be turned off," I said. "Now would you like *me* to do that or would you rather take care of it yourself?"

Her eyes widened. Trying to save herself embarrassment, she muttered, "Mom! Like I don't hear that word—and worse—at school."

"Unfortunately you do," I answered. "But this is not school—this is our home. And you're not going to hear it within these walls. Now, again I ask: Do you want me to turn it off or are you going to take care of it?"

"You really are treating me like a baby."

And Be Diplomatic

She said it in such an uncharacteristically bratty way that I easily could have overreacted. Instead, I had the good sense to wrap her in a bear hug.

"No, I'm treating you with the respect you deserve—exactly the way I expect your friends to treat you," I said. "If I thought you were a baby, I would have thundered in there and turned it off myself. Out of respect for your maturity, I'm giving you the choice."

She went back into the family room and muttered, "Sorry, guys. My mom says we can't watch this."

I expected to hear groans from the group. Instead, one of the boys quickly apologized. "Oh, Holly, I'm sorry. We didn't mean to get you in trouble."

"I'm not in trouble. We just can't watch this."

Yes, give your children a strong shoulder to lean against while they're learning their own balance.

Acquaint Your Kids with Your Work Environment

Including our children in our work—letting them see chunks of the adult world of work—helps them to be less demanding.

Millie often takes her daughters to the office on Saturday while she runs off the financial forecasts for her company. As they help her put the reports into folders for a Monday morning meeting of the board, she tells them why the papers are so important. Not only do her girls see her work environment, but they are also starting to understand how events elsewhere touch their own lives.

Whenever possible, I included Jay and Holly in my article interviews, so they learned early to fade into the background for those few minutes. Not only did they see how I pay bills, but they also met some wonderful people.

One of their favorite adventures while "on assignment" with me occurred in Nashville, Tennessee. I was tacking business onto our vacation and had arranged a magazine interview with someone I had long admired—the late Sarah Cannon, better known to Grand Ole Opry fans as Minnie Pearl.

On our way to meet Mrs. Cannon before her afternoon appearance on the Grand Ole Opry stage, I outlined her career for my teens, even retelling several of her down-home jokes in which she ridiculed her own looks. I explained the origin of those jokes, adding that she'd grown up being called "plain." Of course, to a child "plain" had translated as "ugly."

We waited only a few minutes in the reception area before Mrs. Cannon greeted us warmly. While she and I talked, Jay and Holly sat quietly, watching and listening.

Then, as we stood and thanked her, she took my hand and said in her quiet way, "Now, I want you and the children to sit out on the stage behind me."

Sit on the historic Grand Ole Opry stage? I nearly yelled with glee, but I managed to accept the invitation gracefully. For the next two hours, the three of us sat behind many of the people who had been an important part of my growing up. Then, Mrs. Cannon, waiting behind the curtain for her cue, turned to smile at me as Roy Acuff announced, "Cousin Minnie Pearl!"

After the show, she graciously said good-bye to us and handed me her home phone number, so I could check details for the final

draft of the article. Back at our car, Jay commented on the musi-
cians, but Holly couldn't get over Mrs. Cannon's attractiveness and
wondered why she would tell those awful jokes on herself.

Two weeks later, I made the prearranged call to Mrs.
Cannon's home. I'd been professional all along, but as we said
good-bye, she said in her gentle Southern voice, "Now do give my
regards to your children. Jay and Holly, right?"

I was astonished she had remembered them by name and
said so. She commented, "My dear, they're remarkable children."

Right then I lost my professionalism and started to babble.
"Mrs. Cannon, I have to tell you that after we left you at the
Opry, Holly turned to me and said, 'Mom, she's so pretty!'"

Without missing a beat, Mrs. Cannon said, "Why, she's even
more remarkable than I thought!"

Allow Your Children to Experience the Consequences of Their Actions

Most of us have read the tough-love books telling us we must let
our children experience the consequences of their actions, even
if doing so means our discomfort in watching their discomfort.
Learning by experience is the hard way to learn, but, for some
youngsters, it is the only way.

Ginny had to bite her lip while letting her son spend his
allowance unwisely and then—because she refused to bail him
out—watching him have to sit out several fun activities. She
knew she was teaching him long-term lessons, but it was still
tough to see him miss all the fun with his friends.

She could have rationalized giving him the extra spending
money, especially since he had "already lost so much in life." But
she wisely chose to have them both tough it out, so he would
learn to budget his money better. It took a few rough weeks, but
when he saw that his sorrowful eyes and pleas of "just this once"

weren't working, he started watching his money more carefully.

And I had to let Jay go to school without lunch several times as we were withdrawing from those good-ol'-Mom-will-come-through situations. When he'd been in elementary school, I'd often taken his lunch to him. But when we moved to New York at the beginning of his eighth grade, we agreed I wouldn't take his lunch to school anymore. Only occasionally did I find his lunch still in the refrigerator in the morning. Of course, he'd eat as soon as he got home at 3:00, so I knew his health wasn't in jeopardy.

Bend a Little on Minor, First-Time Offenses

Then the day came when I opened the refrigerator to get my lunch for work and discovered Holly had forgotten hers. Was it fair to treat her with tough love the first time she failed? But if I gave in, wouldn't I be teaching her that she didn't have to worry about being responsible? That Good Ol' Mom would swoop in to rescue her?

I stood in front of the open refrigerator for a long moment, arguing with myself. Finally I decided if this became a habit, we'd deal with it then. I drove to her school, still mentally arguing with the tough-love experts, deciding Holly wasn't a candidate for their techniques just yet. Besides, I was going to suffer more than she would if I left her lunch in the refrigerator.

I arrived at school just a few minutes before her first class began. She and several of her friends were still by their lockers, combing their hair and chatting about the day's plans. Holly turned just as I approached. The look of surprise and pleasure on her face made the trip worth it. She thanked me profusely for bringing her lunch, reminding me she'd made egg salad and had been disappointed to discover she'd left it home.

Our long-standing custom has been to hug good-bye, but after I handed her the lunch and heard one more thank-you, I stood there awkwardly for a moment. I wanted that hug, but I didn't want to embarrass her in front of her friends.

Finally I said, "Well, I've got to head for work. Who wants a hug before I go?"

Kristi hopped up from the floor. "I do!"

I gave her a motherly bear hug, while Holly stood by, red-faced and saying, "Mom!"

Then Jessica said, "Me, too." One by one, I gave her five friends a squeeze to send them into the day. Finally only Holly was left. I hugged her and hurried out the door.

That night, as we cleared the table after dinner, she again thanked me for having taken her lunch to school. I said I hoped I hadn't embarrassed her with all of the hugs.

She shook her head. "You did at first because you're always doing weird things. But later, two of the girls said you're pretty neat. I just agreed with them."

I gave her another big hug right then.

By the way, that was the last time she forgot her lunch.

When Push Comes to Shove, Hang Tough

While it's wonderful to be understanding, forgiving and open to discussing house rules, the time will come when you have to make a decision—and not let yourself be talked out of it. When those moments came for us, Jay and Holly used to argue. But I'd say, "Just write this on your list of 'Rotten Things My Mom Used to Do.' I'll sign it so that you have proof when you show it to some future psychologist."

The argument always ended there.

Then came the year I decided we were going to attend an honest-to-goodness Fourth of July fireworks display. In the past, we'd always been at our lake trailer, and the kiddos had been content with sparklers. But this time I wanted to show them a sky filled with orange and green and red and blue. Okay, so *I* wanted to see a display again.

When I excitedly told them about my plans, they just glanced at each other with a here-we-go-again look. And that afternoon 10-year-old Jay ran into the house. "Mom! Timmy's got a bag of bottle rockets we're gonna shoot off tonight. Isn't that great?!"

I looked up from my mending. "But we're going to the park to see the fireworks. Remember?"

Jay frowned. "I don't wanna go. I wanna shoot bottle rockets."

For several moments I tried to reason with him. Finally I said, "That's enough. I'm pulling rank. You *are* going to the fireworks."

Jay glared at me and then went to his room.

All through dinner, he was sullen. At the park, he ignored my attempts to draw him into the conversation Holly and I were enjoying.

Then I opened the cooler. "What do you want? Cola or juice?" I asked, thinking he'd refuse rather than have to answer.

Instead he mumbled, "Cola."

I bit the inside of my lip to keep from commenting.

At last, the smoke rocket went up to test the degree of darkness. It was followed by an explosion that filled the sky with a brilliant orange umbrella.

As the crowd emitted a collective "ahhhh," Jay turned to me, his eyes sparkling. "Wow, Mom. This is great!"

My wink was the closest I got to saying, "I told you so."

Teach Your Children Responsibility

Counselors and child experts remind us that children who have time on their hands aren't happy. In fact, those who have no chores and no responsibilities tend to quarrel much more than those who have to be busy around the home.

Also, single mothers easily get trapped into thinking we have to juggle *every* ball. But the one labeled "chores" can be easily passed along to the children. And we have the fewest discipline problems when we make sure the kids understand exactly what we expect from them when we assign chores.

Usually we *can't* just say, "Clean your room." We have to give specifics: "Make up your bed. Hang up your clothes. Put away the toys. Dust the dresser, chair and bed."

I reminded myself of that fact many times when I sent Jay back to his room with the instruction that he was to look at the mess through *my* eyes. Let's face it, most teen boys just don't share their mother's obsession with neatness. I had to learn that Jay's room is Jay's room.

My kiddos liked having a list on the kitchen counter so that they could cross off each item as they finished. I found a list worked better than just giving them another chore after they'd finish the first one. If they kept getting a string of chores, they'd be defeated, thinking the work would never end. We all need to see the goal is possible.

I also found that they worked best if I worked with them. So when they were first learning to work, I couldn't just say, "Put all your toys on the shelf." I needed to say, "*Let's* put your toys on the shelf."

Even young children can be in charge of an occasional meal that doesn't require cooking. And there's nothing wrong with cold chicken sandwiches for dinner.

The important thing is that you are spending time together and talking about your day. Meals together can often be the family's cement.

With my entry into single parenting, I didn't cook the way I used to—meat and potatoes on the table every night at 5:30—but

I also refused to give in to the fast-food syndrome. Our meals consisted of a protein and a crunchy vegetable. I also made double portions so that the leftovers—after getting zapped in the microwave—could provide another meal. We'd add a fresh salad, and we had a feast.

One of our dinners each week was always baked chicken. Not only did we get a good meal, but the leftovers also provided several lunches throughout the week. And that was a boon, as I refuse to buy regular lunch meat—it's too expensive and filled with salt and nitrites.

Some good things came out of my busy schedule—Jay and Holly had to take more responsibility in the kitchen. The best system we found was to alternate days of cooking and cleaning—Holly got the even days of the month and Jay got the odd days.

Those first meals the kids put together were rather interesting: Holly enjoyed trying cookbook recipes and trading ideas with her friends, while Jay served whatever was in the refrigerator. But he soon progressed from warmed-over pizza to spicy potatoes and a marvelous cheese-broccoli soup. Today, for company he often prepares a five-course dinner complete with marinated meat, homemade bread and his personalized chocolate dessert cups filled with black raspberry mousse. Ah, perseverance pays off.

So, What About Spanking?

Carl and Marilyn, my Michigan friends with six children, were my parenting mentors long before my own Jay and Holly arrived. Carl said they punished biblically—warn, act, love.

Since we attended the same Sunday School class, we often talked about the challenges of raising children. Carl said he couldn't use grounding as an effective tool with six youngsters, but said that they knew after the paddling, he was going to wrap his arms around them.

His wife, Marilyn, says, "It's neat to see our grown-up kids now making the same decisions with their children we had to make"—such as no Saturday morning cartoons until each child's chores are done.

Proverbs 22:6 says, "Train a child in the way he should go, and when he is old he will not turn from it." Several biblical scholars agree that the original context is "train a child in *his* way," meaning according to what will work for that child. And haven't we seen that what is effective discipline for one child often doesn't even faze another child? What an awesome responsibility. We want to discipline our children but not to the extent that we drive them away from us—and from the Lord.

I used to tell my kiddos I loved them and wanted them to behave in such a way that other folks would like them. So hang in there and know if we make the right decisions now we can relax—a bit—later.

Don't Let Discipline Become Abuse

Be Aware

Child abuse is a growing problem in our society. Whenever the growing statistics are cited, the same reasons are offered—stress, increased pressures, unrealistic expectations on the part of the parent, frustration at the way life has turned out, alcohol and/or drug abuse, lack of an extended family support system or a continuing cycle of abuse from generation to generation. And the potential of abuse is often especially real for single mothers who are trying to juggle too many responsibilities.

I know how thin that line between discipline and abuse is. One day, early in my singlehood, we three were hurrying to get out the door to school and work. As they gulped their cereal, I hurriedly packed their lunch boxes since I'd been too tired the night before.

Then, just as we grabbed our jackets, 10-year-old Jay said, "Oh, I forgot. We're supposed to take our lunches in bags today since we're going to the museum."

I absolutely lost it. I slapped his arm in anger, then yelled about his thoughtlessness as I jerked the food items out of his lunch box and threw them into a bag.

They both watched—and listened—to me in stunned, frightened silence. Big tears welled up in Holly's eyes, and all Jay could say was, "I'm sorry, Mom."

I looked at those two frightened little kids who had no one to depend on except the crazy woman I had just become. I put my hands over my face and sobbed.

And that was exactly the right thing to do. Not only had I had the good sense to look at my children in that crazy scene and release my tension by crying, but that evening I also gave them the assignment of packing their own lunches right after dinner each evening.

Be Prepared

One of the joys of growing older is our ability to finally anticipate those situations that make us feel stressed out and hopeless.

If I'm overly tired or worried about bills or feeling pulled in too many directions, I'm impossible. But I've also learned to say, "I can't handle this well right now," and withdraw until I can cool down. And I know, sooner or later, I'm going to have to talk to the Lord about it, so I try to talk to Him even while I'm still angry or disappointed.

Remember, when He said in Matthew 19:14 (*KJV*), "Come unto me," He *didn't* add, "But come with a smile on your face."

So don't hit your children while you're angry. But if it happens, give yourself time to cool off but don't pretend nothing happened. Then face your kids, apologize, and talk it through.

But don't wring your hands and lament that they have a rotten mother—because they don't!

Maybe you need to tell them what you need from them and what you're willing to offer in return. Sometimes that translates into "When I get home from work, I need at least to get my coat hung up before you spring the latest crisis on me. Give me those few minutes, and I'll be ready to listen closely then."[1]

Serve Discipline with Love

I can't stress enough that discipline must be tempered with lots of love. Children don't read minds any more than we do, so they aren't going to know they are loved unless they experience it through words and action.

One summer, I heard Dr. Gary Chapman, a pastor and counselor from Winston-Salem, North Carolina, speak on the five languages of love. Even though he was talking about husbands and wives seldom speaking the same language, his comments helped me understand Jay and Holly more.

Here are the five ways, he says, folks hear they are loved.

Words. Hearing "I love you," "I appreciate your hard work" and "I'm glad you're part of this family" gives many of us the energy to tackle the next crisis.

Acts of service. The theme song for those of us with this language is "Don't Talk of Love—Show Me!"

Gifts. For many, Holly included, a gift often says, "I saw this and thought of you."

Physical touch. Dr. Chapman says this is the language many husbands hear best. But translating that into a pat on your child's shoulder each time you pass or into a good-bye hug can convey your love, too.

Quality time. The amazing thing about this language is that this person, Jay included, wants to spend time with another but doesn't necessarily need to talk. Suddenly I understood my

Southern relatives who wanted their wives to spend four hours fishing with them, but wouldn't utter three words—unless they were "Move your feet."[2]

Of course, even though most of us speak one or two of these languages, a serving of a little bit of all of these will help us establish an atmosphere in which the children know they are loved even as we keep working on the discipline.

Once More with Feeling

- Know why you discipline your children.
- Have a discipline road map in which you outline specific goals, define your values and establish the firm limits that give your youngsters a sense of security.
- Help build your children's self-esteem and aid their growth toward maturity.
- Reinforce their positive social development by providing suitable group experiences and making their friends welcome in your home.
- Discern whether your kids are being deliberately disobedient or simply caving in to peer pressure when they break agreed-upon rules.
- Acquaint your kids with your work environment to enhance their appreciation of your responsibilities and to broaden their horizons.
- Allow them to experience the natural consequences of repeated action.
- Be flexible when incidents involve first-time, minor offenses.
- But when push comes to shove, hang tough.
- Teach your children responsibility and keep them from idleness through assigned chores.

- Punish biblically—warn, act, love—but don't allow discipline to become abuse.
- Always serve up discipline with generous amounts of love.

Notes

1. By the way, for information and referrals of local protective agencies, you can write to: The National Committee for Prevention of Child Abuse, P.O. Box 2866, Chicago, IL 60690. Or call the National Child Abuse Hotline: 1-800-4-A-CHILD.

   To report child abuse locally, you can call the child protective agency in your county. Don't just close your eyes to what is happening to children. They need both the protection and discipline of loving adults.

2. Gary D. Chapman, Ph.D., *The Five Love Languages* (Chicago: Northfield Publishing, 1992), n.p.

CHAPTER NINE

We Love Our Kin, but We'll Raise Our Kids

*Do not forsake your friend and the friend of your father, and do not
go to your brother's house when disaster strikes you—better a neighbor
nearby than a brother far away.*

PROVERBS 27:10

Remember Aesop's fable about the man who tried to please everyone? He and his son were on their way to market, leading their donkey and enjoying the beautiful morning together.

One of their neighbors saw them and said, "Now isn't that silly? You have a fine donkey with you, but both of you are walking."

So the father set his son on the donkey, and they continued toward the market.

But after a few minutes, another friend saw them and said to the son, "How rude you are to ride while your old father must walk."

So the father joined the child on the donkey's back. It wasn't long, though, until they passed a third friend.

"How thoughtless you are," he said, "to make this poor donkey carry both of you to town."

So they both slid off the donkey, and the father promptly picked up the animal and put it across his shoulders.

As they slowly walked along, a fourth neighbor saw them. "Well, that's the silliest thing I've ever seen—a donkey being carried."

The obvious moral is that we can't please everyone. May we apply that same philosophy to our single parenting.

We Will Care for the Children

When I made the conscious decision not to marry again—contrary to the comments and advice of my relatives—I also made the decision I would raise Jay and Holly to the best of my ability—alone. Again, my decision ran contrary to the expectations of my relatives.

A typical Kentuckian, my dad was a teller of tales, and most of his accounts of life in the hills were filled with high drama. I grew up listening, horrified and in tears, to epics of a neighbor who murdered his wife, of children who were given away or of fires that consumed wooden houses within minutes.

But the story he told of an ancestor's refusal to accept his second wife's children always stirred my temper rather than my tears.

The relative's first wife had died, leaving him with three youngsters. Grief and reality often walked together in the hills at the turn of the century, so within a matter of weeks, he was looking for another wife to take care of his children. The prime candidate was a widow with three young boys. They married quickly, and the boys were sent to live with the woman's brother in a neighboring town.

When the mule-drawn wagon with the three boys in it started down the lane and away from the only house they knew as home, the youngest began to scream out, "Mama! Mama!"

When Dad mentioned the little boy's grief at being separated from his mother, I went berserk.

"How could she give up her children like that?"

"What do you mean?" Dad asked. "The house was too small for three more boys."

"But not too small for the ones he and she had together afterward! I'd be cussed before I'd give up my children like that!"

"What would you do?" he'd ask. "There you are stuck in the hills with three young'ns, living off other people's charity."

At 17, I had more fight than sense. But I also had mother bear instincts, and I knew even then I'd fight for my cubs.

"We'd walk to the nearest town even if it took days," I said. "I'd find work or I'd walk the streets, but I'd feed my children. And no man on this earth would take 'em from me! She was spineless for giving hers up, and he was scum for making her do so!"

Neither of us ever won over the other when it came to airing our views on those ancestors and their kids. In fact, that argument between Dad and me was two decades old when I became a single parent. Suddenly, though, my dad derived comfort from my long-standing position. He knew I would take good care of my children—his grandchildren.

We Are Still in Charge

Not only do relatives often expect us to act a certain way, but those expectations also easily fall on our children. Two days after my husband's funeral, his dad said good-bye to us in our kitchen.

As he hugged 10-year-old Jay, he said, "Take care of your mother. You're the man of the house now."

I was standing where I could see Jay's face, and I was struck by the panic that flashed across his eyes.

I looked at his grandfather. "No, Dad. He's the 10-year-old son in this house."

Jay has since commented at how much it meant to him when I said that. He'd just lost one parent; he needed the security of knowing his mom was in charge.

Actually, expecting inappropriate adult action and responsibility from our children is an area we single mothers have to watch. Yes, it's tempting to treat our children as our confidants, but they are the children and we are the parent.

We Will Decide What's Best for Them

After Karen became single again, her father-in-law started complaining about her keeping the two children in a Christian school and, as he said, "shielding them from the real world." She was convinced that keeping them in that school was what was best for the children for the coming year. So like Hannah in 1 Samuel 1:15—when the priest Eli accused her of being drunk—she quietly answered the charges. She said, "But I'm the one who's responsible for them. I'm the one who must stand before God and give an account."

Later, she talked with a trusted friend about her frustrations, saying through her tears, "It's a bigger issue than just the public or private school matter. It's the whole thing of whether I know what's best for *my* two children."

I can identify with that feeling, because some of my relatives had quiet fits when I took an editorial job in New York. They'd never been there themselves; they had only seen movies of New York City. But they told me I was taking my children into one of the world's roughest spots.

As it turned out, only the financial part was rough. I loved the cloistering tree branches that hung over the road there and the gentle rolling hills that reminded me of my own beloved Kentucky. And I was especially pleased with the schools.

So I shrugged off the relatives' comments. By the time I'd decided to move away from their cocoon, I'd stopped trying to please them.

We Won't Worry Anymore About Fitting an Image

I guess I knew I shouldn't have cared quite so much about what all the relatives thought. But for a long while I did.

It's been difficult to swim against the emotional tide—and standards—they set for me during those early years when I was growing up. Besides, adults are just tall children, and there's enough little kid in me that I've always wanted my extended family to be proud of me.

Trying to Fit My Relatives' Image

When I was growing up within my Southern culture, I was supposed to learn to care for a future family. That translated into planting enormous vegetable gardens, canning and freezing the produce, sewing my own clothing and making quilts from the leftover fabric. Those are certainly admirable skills, but they didn't mesh with my determination to go to college and become a teacher.

Naturally, at the obligatory clan gatherings, I felt like a misfit as an occasional uncle commented on my getting "too proper" or one of many aunts pointedly praised her daughter's latest sewing project before asking what I was working on. Gradually, I got it into my head I wouldn't be a "real woman" until I made my own quilt.

So, within a week of graduation from college, I purchased a kit for a white quilt top to be embroidered with shades of blue before being quilted in a scroll pattern with several thousand tiny stitches. I worked on it, off and on, while I completed my master's degree and produced two babies. Finally, six years later, the day came when my quilt was finished. .

I invited my Kentucky grandmother, Mama Farley, my mother and two of my aunts for an official showing that would declare my womanly status at last. I spread the quilt across a double bed and stood back, awaiting their verdict.

Mama Farley smiled. "Oh, Honey, that's pretty. That's just about the prettiest quilt I've ever—"

She stopped in midsentence as she turned back the corner of the quilt to examine its underside. Then suddenly, she let it fall back onto the bed.

"Oh! Knots!" was all she would say.

Why hadn't I remembered that the knotted thread must always be pulled into the inside of the quilt? I hadn't, so I still wasn't a "real" woman.

I had no choice but to try again. For my next quilt, I chose a pink dogwood pattern to be appliquéd onto a white background. That one took me nine years of sewing tiny stitches as I taught, raised children, wrote books, nursed my husband through numerous cancer battles, grieved his death and, later, moved my children to New York for my career change.

One Saturday morning, I finished the pink binding and knotted the last of the pink thread—remembering to tuck it inside. Jay and Holly were at an overnight youth activity, so, alone in our small condo and 800 miles away from any relatives, I spread the quilt onto my bed, turned back the corner to check for knots and pronounced myself a real woman—at long last!

Learning to Keep My Eyes on the Lord

Actually, by then, the ceremony had lost its earlier meaning because my having survived several of life's traumas of grief and a career change had already convinced me I wasn't quite as worthless as I had once thought. I was learning to release my low self-esteem to the Lord and to latch onto Philippians 3:13-14: "But one thing I do: Forgetting what is behind and straining toward what is ahead, I press on toward the goal to win the prize for which God has called me heavenward in Christ Jesus."

Oh, I've hit a few bumpy spots in the process, but I've learned along the way what is really important: to keep my eyes on Him and off the impossible task of fitting the images and expectations of others.

By the way, even my quilt victory was short lived. After I told this story publicly, one of the women in my audience told me neither quilt "counted" since they both were from kits. See what I mean about the impossibility of pleasing others?

Just Ignoring the Demands of Others

I wish I'd had Amy's creativity that first year when I was trying to juggle emotions and schedule adjustments along with the relatives' demands. Rather than dwelling on the notions of what others think she should do, she reads her personal list of what kind of mom she can be, given her circumstances and the needs of her child, and then she reminds herself of what God has called her to do and to be. Thus, she is accountable to her heavenly Father rather than trying to be super woman or to fit another person's ideal. Making—and reading often—a list like that is a perfect way to face the new day and the latest challenge.

I wish I'd done that instead of pouring out my frustration to long-time friends, Dan and Janet. But Dan listened in his quiet way, and then gave me the best advice any single parent could have: "Walk in God's light and pay no attention to what anyone else says."

Once More with Feeling

- As a single mom raising kids alone, you can't hope to satisfy the expectations of all your relatives, so don't even try.
- You, not they, someday will stand before God to give an account for your parenting, so resist their attempts to pressure you in directions that are not best for you and the children.
- Stand firm in your decision to care for your children and to decide what is best for them.
- Don't make things worse with an offending relative by arguing. Remember the truth of Proverbs 15:1: "A gentle answer turns away wrath, but a harsh word stirs up anger."
- In the absence of their father, you must protect your small children from feeling unduly burdened. They need the security of knowing Mom is still in charge.
- Remember to keep your eyes on Him and off the impossible task of fitting the images and expectations of others.
- Remind yourself often of the kind of mom you can be, given your circumstances and the needs of your child.
- Walk in God's light, and pay no attention to what all the rest are saying.
- Listen to the Lord, and you'll find that He drowns out the voices of opinionated relatives.

CHAPTER TEN

When the Kids Fight

How good and pleasant it is when brothers live together in unity!

PSALM 133:1

Jay and Holly used to have the most ridiculous arguments. One day, I'd just gotten home from work when they stormed into my bedroom.

"Mom, ground Holly," Jay demanded. "She threw stuff at me!"

"Holly," I asked, "what did you throw at him?"

"String," she conceded.

I sighed and looked at Jay. "What's the big deal? So she threw string at you."

He never batted an eye. "Mom, it was on a wooden *spool.*"

Hang In There

We single mothers have enough crises to juggle without having to referee within our own homes. But having children at odds often happens.

I remember all too well the tension Jay and Holly—"the greatest kids in the world"—went through as both often wished each were an only child. And there were moments when, if they'd kept it up, I could have accommodated either wish very easily!

At times, I was convinced they stayed awake nights, thinking up ways to aggravate each other. That started just about puberty—and it was an exhausting time.

For a while, they were so rude to each other I was tempted not to write this book. One exhausting afternoon I listened to another round of "Did not. Did, too" until I said, "Boy, my editor ought to hear this. How can I write about single parenting when you guys don't get along?"

Jay barely glanced my way. "Just have a chapter called 'When the Kids Fight.'"

I shook my head. "But we've been through so much together! And we've got enough battles outside; we don't need to face more *inside* these walls! We've got to get through this as friends!"

Simultaneously, they looked at each other and laughed. So much for manipulation by guilt.

It Will Get Better

Having Rules Helps Some

When their quarreling first appeared, I had two rules.

Rule One: No battles—either physically or verbally.

Rule Two: You don't have to like one another, but you do have to respect each other.

They didn't always stick to those rules, but just knowing I expected that behavior helped keep them on track. I'm convinced youngsters will eventually meet our expectations, so I tried to say encouraging things such as "You're a neat kid. I'm surprised you said anything that mean."

But Their Maturity Helps Most

By the time they hit their late teens, they were friends again. In fact, one afternoon as Holly and I ran errands, she said, "You know, Mom, Jay's really neat. I like talking to him."

I almost wrecked the car as I whipped around to see who'd said that.

As my kids got older, they wonderfully moved past the constant bickering. They talked, double-dated and even ran errands together. Often I stood by the front window, waving good-bye and marveling at the miracle of their friendship.

How Did It Happen?

If I knew *exactly*, I'd go on a sold-out lecture tour.

Oh, I want to take credit and say my involvement with my teens, my demand for mutual respect and our constant communication brought us to this refreshing understanding. But, in reality, their maturity had more to do with it than anything else.

When Do Kids Fight?

If your children are still little, when do they argue? Always, of course, when it's the most inconvenient or awkward for you. Kids can square off anytime at the drop of a hat, but the following times seem to rank among their favorites for sparring with one another.

Whenever the Phone Rings

Every mother knows that as soon as the phone rings and she goes to answer it, kids look at each other and say, "What can we get into? I know; let's fight."

One young mother keeps special games by the phone—and the children can play with these games only when she's on the phone. That's solved a big problem.

Just Before the Evening Meal

Others have discovered their kids fight in the hour before dinner. Sheila has a system now that as soon as she gets home from work, her youngsters can make the dinner salads and eat those right away. Some moms keep sliced carrots and quartered apples handy.

Yes, it takes time to make sure those items are available but—since most kids prefer eating to arguing—it keeps the children from feuding and lets the moms change out of their work clothes without first having to referee another unscheduled bout.

When You're the Most Tired

With my kids, it seemed the biggest arguments started when I was the most tired. To keep from yelling, I would ask them to suggest their own solutions for the current difficulty.

Holly's suggestions were invariably the most reasonable, and Jay's were always the most dramatic. But, between them, they usually managed to get us through the crisis of the moment.

More on this point later.

And Always in the Car

My two youngsters have vastly differing tastes in music, so it seemed that as soon as we had finished praying for journeying mercies but before we had left the driveway, they were already arguing over the radio stations.

My standard solution was uncreative, but it worked. "If you two can't agree on what station to listen to, you'll just have to listen to the one I want."

They quickly learned listening to my music was worse than listening to each other's, so they compromised.

Why Kids Fight

They're Trying to Establish Their Own Identity

I've found teens are often at odds with their parents because they're trying to pull away from the family unit to establish their own identity. That's tension enough, but add a sibling or two going through their own crises and you've got the potential for a battle.

They're Feeling They Don't Have a Voice in Anything That Happens

Part of the frustration of being a child is not having a voice in anything that happens. This feeling is particularly strong in a child who is expected to take care of all the others.

Patty remembers having to care for three younger brothers and never feeling as though she had a voice in anything happening in her life. No wonder she couldn't wait to get out of that house. And sadly, she isn't close to any of her family members now.

When her mother wants to have the whole family together at holidays, Patty tries to avoid it, thinking, *I had enough of that when I lived with them.*

How to Keep the War Going

Yell a Lot

When they're arguing again, the easy thing to do is yell, "Shut up!" but that merely increases the tension—and the volume.

Go for Guilt

One thing that doesn't work with kids is trying to make them feel guilty for not liking each other. Sue remembers her mother saying, "Just think if something happened to your brother and sister." She says she thought about that a lot.

When my kids argued, I'd remind them that no one else on this earth shares the same memories that the two of them do.

"Years from now," I'd say, "No one else will know how you got Petey Cat; no one else will remember the guy Jay nicknamed "Fredetals"; no one else will have shared the same experiences with our zany relatives."

Did it work? No. They still rolled their eyes. But at least I felt better.

Set Up Competition

A principle every parent in the world knows but doesn't always follow is *don't set up competition,* especially the kind that turns kids into adversaries. We know we have enough problems without pitting our children against each other, so we think, *I'd never do that.*

But even saying something as seemingly innocent as, "Let's see who is Mommy's best helper," while you and the children pick up their toys creates competition. Unintentionally, you make the children rivals, not for a prize but for Mommy's favor and approval.

Make Comparisons

Grades are a common problem area, and more than one adult still remembers hearing, "Why can't you get good grades like your sister?"

I confess I often wished Jay had more of Holly's neatness. But I tried to stay out of comparisons. Once a much-younger Holly said, "I bet you wish Jay was neat like me, huh, Mom?"

I fought the impulse to say "Yes!" Instead, while I praised her sense of organization, I also pointed out some of Jay's good qualities: "Holly, I'm glad you keep your room neat. That helps give me a sense of peace and harmony. Jay doesn't keep his room that way, but I do appreciate his painting the kitchen perfectly and without my having to bug him."

If you have a less-than-neat kid, too, be encouraged that the chances are good he or she *will* grow out of it.

How to Win a Cease-Fire

Involve Them in the Solutions
Since the biggest arguments seemed to start when I was the most tired, I usually asked the kiddos for their own suggestions: "How would you solve this if you were the mom and I was the child?"

Holly always suggested reasonable solutions. "I guess I'd send us to separate rooms until we can decide to get along."

Jay would be dramatic. "No, remind us how difficult it is to raise kids alone. Remind us you didn't run away to Tahiti or to Kentucky when Dad died, and tell us how that relative gave her children up when she remarried. And we'll remind you that her youngest boy wouldn't go to his mother's funeral years later."

By the time he'd finished, I was usually laughing so hard that the tension was gone from the situation.

When Keri asked her 10-year-old son how he'd solve their argument, she was surprised to hear, "I'd ask the kid what had happened at school today to make him so grouchy."

Give Each Separate Time
With two totally different children, I found that spending separate weekend evenings together worked for us. So, while Holly babysat, Jay and I usually went out for hamburgers and talked. Then while Jay was at work, Holly and I shopped or chatted over quiche at our favorite tea shop.

I shared my idea with a young friend who promptly told me families are stronger if they do things together—always. I also noticed neither of her children was even five years old yet!

But the separate times worked for us. Just as children need personal space—whether it's a room or just a brightly colored "secrets" box—they need to have their parent for a few minutes that belong just to them alone. In fact, if children know they'll have uninterrupted time later, they're less apt to be so demanding beforehand.

Treat Them as Individuals

As their mother, I tried to treat Jay and Holly fairly and equally. But I couldn't treat them the same, because they aren't the same.

When Jay has a problem, he wants to be left alone until he's worked it out mentally. Holly, on the other hand, likes to discuss every detail of her decision-making process. As a teen, by the time she'd made her decision, we were both tired.

Sure, it's exhausting trying to treat children as individuals, but so is trying to undo the damage from raising cookie-cutter kids.

And speaking of equality: Do your children ever argue about which one should get the larger half of the last piece of cake? Mine did as youngsters—until I heard a veteran mother say she solved the problem by having one child cut the coveted item and then giving the other child first choice.

Get It in Writing

Just as the contract Holly had written about dating got me out of many rough spots, so have the other contracts the kids and I have drawn up concerning curfew, grades and social life. Not only did the written words clarify any misunderstandings, but they also helped me remember what I'd said.

Achieve an Armistice with Prayer

Several years ago, it'd been another one of those frustrating days when I didn't need to face two warring teens. As soon as I hit the door, though, they both wanted to tell their side of the story—namely whose turn it was to get the TV.

Understanding mother that I am, I spouted something close to "You guys must hold secret meetings at night to see how you can drive me nuts!" I didn't even have my coat off yet, but we sat on the carpeted stairs as I listened to one side and then to the other. Then I mumbled, "I gotta pray about this."

Still on the stairs, I started with a simple "Father, I hate days like this. I identify more with Saul's craziness than Solomon's wisdom, so please show me how to solve this."

Jay and Holly didn't offer to pray then, and I didn't make them. They needed space and time to think. I sent them to their rooms, said they couldn't watch TV for the rest of the evening and added that I didn't want to see them until dinner, 30 minutes later. We'd work out a schedule then.

At a mothers' luncheon some time later, I shared my honest prayer. Afterward, another mother scolded me for *not* making my children pray aloud right then. She declared she does that all the time and her children never even raise their voices in the house.

She also let me know if I were a truly spiritual mother, my children would have done the right thing immediately.

I asked her how old her children are.

"Six and nine," she answered.

I patted her arm. "That's wonderful," I said.

But what I meant was "Let's talk again in about seven years."

Keep Working for Peace

Truthfully, I didn't want my children to be obedient little robots. I wanted children who were learning how to work through problems and who would see God as their heavenly Father to whom they can always go, whether they're hurting or happy.

Maybe, just maybe, by seeing me turn to the Lord for solutions, my kiddos learned He's ready to listen to anything.

Once More with Feeling

- Hang in there; it will get better. Having rules helps some; but the children's own maturity—which takes time to achieve—helps most.
- Don't be surprised when your kids seem to pick the most awkward times to have their arguments. In fact, you can count on it.
- Watch to see when your children argue most. Once you've identified those times, find creative ways to head them off.
- Driving you crazy is seldom your kids' intent when they fight. More often, they're trying to establish their own identities, or they may be feeling they don't have any say in what is going on around them.
- You can keep your youngsters fighting by such counterproductive steps as yelling a lot, going for guilt, creating competition and constantly making comparisons between the kids.
- Listen to your children's complaints. You may see another facet of the problem.
- Involve them in the solutions to their problems. Even an off-the-wall suggestion may provide the right result.
- Give each child time alone with you. Knowing they can count on those uninterrupted minutes when you are entirely theirs adds peace to the household.
- Do treat your children as individuals with separate interests and different needs. They are not the same, so you can't treat them the same, even though you are being fair and giving each one equal consideration.
- Pray honestly for them and with them.

· As your children see you turn to the Lord for solutions, they will learn to see God as their heavenly Father to whom they also can go, whether they're hurting or happy.

CHAPTER ELEVEN

Help, When I Tied My Son's Tie, He Turned Blue!

I thank my God every time I remember you.

PHILIPPIANS 1:3

Several years ago on a church trip, Jay, Holly and I shared a bus with a group visiting from Mexico City. We couldn't communicate with them, but we smiled and nodded at each other, as our guides explained the various historical sights.

It was a long day, and by the time our bus stopped for dinner, I was exhausted. As we lined up for the washroom, I rested my arms on top of Holly's head, thinking of the day's endless activities.

I had been cheated in a souvenir purchase. I had momentarily lost Jay twice. I had tripped over Holly all day—she insisted on being as close as possible because of the new and, to her, frightening scenes. Basically, I thought I'd made a mistake in taking the trip. Soon my thoughts escalated into conviction that single parenting was an insurmountable challenge, too. Inwardly, I cried, *Lord, I can't do this!*

Right at that moment, one of the Mexican grandmothers stopped in front of me, patted my arm and said in her halting English, "You good mama."

It was just as though God Himself stepped in to say, "Oh, stop. You *can* do this because I am with you."

Suddenly, I wasn't quite so tired.

Trusting Those We Love to God

When Jay was a toddler and his sister just three months old, I had to run some errands. Everything had gone fairly well, even with the baby in my left arm, my purse slung over my shoulder, the purchases in my left hand and 20-month-old Jay clutched with my right.

As we approached the escalator, I let go of Jay for just a second to steady myself. Quickly I reached for him, but he stepped back, unsure of getting on anything that moved. The escalator was taking me away as he stood watching. Before I had a chance to panic, though, an older couple walked up behind Jay.

"Please grab his hand," I said. The couple nodded and brought my smiling little boy with them. They were there when I couldn't be.

That's what I continue to trust the Lord for as I pray—that He will supply the right people or the right experiences to grab hold of the person for whom I'm interceding. And as I pray, I'm remembering the older couple that "just happened" to appear at the precise moment I needed them. God does care. And we do not pray to air. That's what I hang on to when the doubts creep in.

We All Need Each Other

Yes, that couple was there when I needed help, but I've had other times when I was the one who supplied the help— such as when I was on my long-ago church trip to the Middle East.

In Old Jerusalem, the cavelike shops with their piles of spices and fruits, camel rugs and rows of carved manger scenes delighted me. But it was the people who interested me most. We bumped against one another in the narrow passageways, my murmured "Sorry" falling on ears that comprehended no English.

Just in front of the slabs of beef and lamb in the open-air meat market, I saw a young Palestinian mother. Cradled in her left arm was a baby, just a few months old. With her right hand, she was steering a little boy who was about three years old. Even though her long gray-green dress and white head scarf announced her different culture, I thought of my own days of juggling two babies and several purchases.

Just then a collective groan went up as the people began moving to the sides of the street. That's when I saw the garbage tractor inching toward us. The streets were already crowded— how could the driver get the tractor through here?

But still I moved aside with the crowd, muttering my usual "Sorry." The unrelenting tractor advanced upon us, forcing us to flatten ourselves—four deep on each side—against the storefronts and each other. Slowly, it began to crawl past us, its over-sized tires only millimeters from my back.

Suddenly someone was pummeling my legs. The little son of the Palestinian mother was trying to fight his way past me—and into the path of that awful tractor with its load of garbage.

I grabbed his shoulder and looked beyond the tractor to where I had last seen the young mother, knowing the panic she must feel. She also was trapped against the wall, clutching the baby close to her face to keep the child from being crushed. But while she was protecting the one, her eyes were darting over the crowd for the other who had been separated from her in the pushing.

Still gripping her little son's shoulder with one hand, I waved to her with the other while her little boy clung to my tired knees and kicked my ankles for all he was worth.

"He's here. I have him here with me!" I shouted.

Her bewildered stare let me know she didn't understand me, and all of us were pressed too tightly together for me to pick the child up for her to see. All I could do was point dramatically toward my feet and smile, hoping she understood her son was safe.

At last, with the garbage tractor safely past us, I could steer the child to his anxious mother. As he recognized her skirt, he clutched it, sobbing with relief. I touched his dark hair and looked into the brown, misty eyes of his mother as she nodded her thanks to me.

I wanted to tell her about my two children. But we couldn't talk; we merely looked at one another through our tear-filled eyes. I touched her little boy's head once more and then slipped back into the throng of shoppers.

I had been there for that mother's child during a time of crisis. And we, as single parents, quickly learn we need others to be there for our children, too.

And We All Need Help

Help Can Come from the Lord
I've noticed when I ask the Lord for a pat on the back, He's quick to give it. But not always in the way I expect.

I remember one Michigan Saturday that wasn't going well at all. I was having trouble balancing the checkbook, and my mechanic had just informed me that the rocker arm—whatever that is—on the car had to be replaced.

I wanted to run away but settled for taking the three of us out for hamburgers. As we walked into the restaurant, I saw that one of my former students—I'll call her Donna—was a waitress there.

Oh, good, I thought sarcastically, *I'm tired and discouraged, and I run into one of the most obnoxious students I've had in 15 years of teaching.* I could still see her in the front row of fifth-hour classical mythology, arms folded and eyes daring me to make the lesson interesting.

But I wasn't going to disappoint Jay and Holly by going to another restaurant. I decided I'd just pretend I hadn't seen her. *Well, Lord, just keep us from being seated in her section, please,* I prayed inwardly.

And where did the hostess lead us? Right to Donna's section, of course. *Any place but here,* I told myself. But just as I opened my mouth to ask for a booth near the window, Donna spotted us and came rushing over.

"Mrs. Aldrich! This is so neat!"

Sure, it'll be easier to poison me this way, I thought. But outwardly, I managed a feeble smile.

"Guess what!" she said. "I'm a Christian now!"

I stood there dumbstruck as my mouth dropped open.

Donna just kept bubbling on. "My sister got saved at college," she said. "And it bugged me that she was always witnessing to me. Then I'd go to your class, and you'd compare the Bible to what the Greeks believed, and I'd get angry all over again.

"But I couldn't get what you said out of my mind. And last year, I got saved! Isn't that neat?"

I was too choked up to talk, so I gave her a hug.

Help Can Come from the Church

We can't always depend on our families to provide the encouragement we need, especially if we live a thousand miles away from them. And, by this time, many of our friends may be hurting from the same circumstances.

A good church is the only thing that's going to see our kids through the rough times. Oh, we have no guarantee church involvement will keep them out of trouble, but our chances for survival are much better.

When we moved to Colorado Springs, our furniture wasn't due to arrive until Monday. But the Sunday before—and only two days after we arrived in town—we were in church.

I'd already talked to several people about the local churches. We'd been in a small fellowship in New York that had provided exactly the sense of family we needed. But with our new move we wanted a bigger church that could offer a wider range of activities.

I quietly checked on the youth leaders, but one of my California friends, Patricia, was more direct after her divorce. She went to the youth minister at their church and told him he had a marvelous opportunity to make a difference in her then nine-year-old son's life. She asked if he was willing to accept the challenge.

He was, and for the next several years he and her son, Kelly, met often for Saturday breakfast. Patricia credits him for helping steer a lonesome boy through the difficult teen years. But none of that would have happened if she hadn't gathered the courage to tell someone what she needed.

Help Can Come from the Kids

Youngsters also can lighten their mom's load—in their own way. A young Jay heard me tell a friend I'd appreciate her prayers as the date of what would have been my twentieth wedding anniversary loomed.

The kiddos' dad had promised for the "Big Two-O" to ask me to marry him, so I dreaded facing that lonely time.

You see, Don had never asked me to marry him. Years ago, when we were still students, he had simply *told* me we were getting married at semester break. And we did.

On the night of that special anniversary, after Jay and Holly went to bed, I worked at my desk. Soon Jay meandered into my office, stammered another "Good night, Mom" and wandered out. Within five minutes, he had done that twice more.

Finally, I said, "Jay, what *is* it?"

He shuffled from one foot to the other in that embarrassed way common to young teens.

At last he blurted, "Mom, will you marry my dad?"

Softly, I answered, "You bet I will, Jay."

I finally could say I had been asked.

Chloe's 14-year-old daughter, Abby, prepared a lovely meatball dinner the night of what would have been her parent's fifteenth anniversary. As her 12-year-old brother, Zach, held the chair for their astonished mother, Abby gave a little speech:

"Even though you and Dad are divorced, Zach and I are glad you met. After all, you had us! So, thanks!"

When Zella refused to get the abortion her boyfriend demanded, he left the state—leaving no forwarding address. She gave birth in the county hospital and worked two jobs throughout her son's school years to support them. When he graduated with honors, he held his diploma high and shouted, "This is because of you, Mom!"

She cried with joy throughout the rest of the ceremony.

Help Can Come from Neighbors and Friends

When we still lived in Michigan, Jay had to wear a tie for his spring concert. Neither one of us had the foggiest notion how to tie a four-in-hand, so I asked a neighbor to teach him. The neighbor did, bless him, and Jay was set for his concert.

I heard of a young mother who was having trouble potty training her two-year-old son. Her husband was in the army, and her male relatives lived miles away. There was no one to give the little guy an example of how to tackle this latest milestone. So she confided to her neighbor and, with some embarrassment, stammered her request for help.

As a result, each evening for the next couple of weeks, she took her son to the neighbor's house, so the husband could give the little fellow a lesson. It worked!

Dr. James Dobson has another idea: drop colored ice cubes in the toilet bowl and encourage the little guy to fire away. Colored cereal pieces work, too!

Help Can Come from the Experts

When Jay turned 13, I was struggling with finding the balance between letting him have fun and forcing him to be, as he put it, "a wimp."

The scene was one of those this-business-of-raising-kids-alone-is-tough episodes. We were at Lake Michigan, and Jay came in all excited about this wonderful new game he, Erik and Andy had of jumping out of a moving boat.

Horrified, I gave the typical, teary-eyed mother arguments about the danger of what he was doing. But he said he could "handle it."

At that point, I launched into an account of Steve, a brilliant former student, who had been killed in a freak accident at his college. I even told about one of our distant relatives who had been killed by his own boat motor after he fell into the lake. I pulled out every horror story I'd ever heard.

Still, Jay remained insistent that he and his friends would be fine. I was just worrying too much, he told me.

Then in a sudden burst of inspiration, I called the Coast Guard, explained the situation and asked if I was overreacting. The officer assured me I wasn't and said not only were the boys' activities stupid, but they were also a good way to get killed.

I asked if he'd tell Jay what he had just told me.

"Yes, put him on," he answered. "I'm tired of pulling bodies out of the lake."

Jay accepted the phone grudgingly and with a teen's greeting of "Yeah?"

I heard the officer's sharp retort even though I couldn't hear his words. Immediately Jay sat straighter.

"Uh, I mean, yes, sir!"

For the next several minutes, Jay listened, and occasionally nodded. Finally, he signed off with a "Okay. Thank you—sir."

I never received the details of the conversation, but as far as I know, the boys didn't play the game again.

That call may very well have saved young teens' lives. Sometimes we have to do the hard thing for the future good of a youngster—whether it's calling a counselor or the police.

It's ironic—and maddening at times—but kids often will receive counsel from others that they will not accept from their parents. You know how that goes: Good ol' Mom's nice to have around sometimes, but really, what does she know?

So whatever the need is and whenever it's necessary, don't be afraid to bring in the heavy artillery.

But Help Comes Only When We Ask

Whatever our need, we must stop waiting for others to anticipate and fill it. They don't read minds any more easily than we do. So, instead of whining, "Nobody understands how rough I have it," we must ask for specific help from our church, from a friend, from whomever when we need it.

Remember, if you don't ask, the answer is *always* no.

In the early days of our singlehood, it's often difficult to find the balance between letting friends help and leaning on them. Still, I remember well-meaning friends who said, "Call me if you need anything," I failed to do so.

Why?

I had so many needs I didn't know where to begin. I wish I'd been able to verbalize my needs *then*.

Here's what I would have liked to have said.

Pray for me. I may appear strong, but the load of single parenting and career juggling is heavy. If I'm new to this role, I'm struggling with unfamiliar territory and need all the help I can get.

If the Lord gives you specific direction, please listen. He knows my needs—whether it's for help with grocery money or for someone to take my son to the Father-Son Banquet at church.

Talk to me. When you see me in church, please offer a sincere greeting. If my children are small, I'm especially hungry for adult conversation. I often feel awkward in church, and your smile and greeting on Sunday morning will make a big difference.

When you ask how I am, please hang around for the answer. If you'll take an interest, even for a few minutes, in what I'm doing, I won't feel so alone—and I won't be so demanding of your time.

And please remember that accepting a divorced person isn't the same as condoning divorce.

Extend common courtesy to me. At a banquet, please don't ask me to move to another table because you and your husband want to sit at a particular table. Yes, my being alone creates an awkward space at the table, but your request is not only rude, it tells me that in the eyes of others, my seating preference doesn't count. That makes me feel like a second-class citizen and increases my feeling of isolation even more.

And please don't talk about your couples' gatherings in front of me. I may be reading the bulletin board in the cloakroom, but I'm also hearing you.

Offer me practical help. Some churches have the well-meaning program of "Adopt a Family," but I don't want to be someone's Christian responsibility. I just want to be treated normally.

Simply invite us into your home just as you would any other family. And please accept when I invite your family to my home.

If my children are young, it would be great if you'd offer to take them shopping for my Christmas present.

Some churches have auto clinic days where single moms can bring their cars for tune-ups, oil changes or winterizing. Other churches keep a file of handymen who are available to help around the house. (Many of the churches wisely ask their men to go to the homes in teams of two.)

Include my children in your outings. The only "normal" family my children will see is yours. What a wonderful ministry you can have just by letting them join you for a family camp-out or church family night.

Many young boys—and girls—have no idea what godly fathers do since they either don't remember their dad or never see him make wise decisions. Start praying now for a godly mentor whose wisdom will provide that needed example.

Talk to my children. Even a two-minute conversation with my son in the hallway will make him look forward to coming to church. You don't have to include him with your family—though what a blessing that would be. But those few minutes each week will make him feel special.

I remember one man who gave 11-year-old Jay an electronic game. That was thoughtful, of course, but he didn't need a toy. He needed a man who would talk to him.

And don't discount the importance of just a few minutes. When I was 12 years old, the course of my life was changed in a

5-minute meeting with my elderly neighbor's niece, Doris Schumacher. Doris taught English and social studies in Minneapolis, and by her example she showed me that education would be my key to a bright future.

What a marvelous mission field—to have a life-changing influence on a child.

Once More with Feeling

- Not only do we all need each other, but we all also need help.
- Ask the Lord for help and encouragement, but don't limit Him.
- The Lord can send help from many sources—from others He will direct to you, even your own kids.
- Get into a good church. The family of God is also your family. Even a few hours each week with other people who love the Lord will make a difference in your family.
- Involve the experts—teachers, counselors and even police—if you need help.
- Help usually comes only when we ask for it. So tell concerned people what you need—whether it's a need for specific prayer, for instructions in tie knotting, for adult conversation or for practical help with your teen.

CHAPTER TWELVE

Counting Wrinkles, Celebrating Joys, Anticipating Life

Teach us to number our days aright, that we may gain a heart of wisdom.

PSALM 90:12

On our tenth wedding anniversary, I gave my husband the companion pictures of an old couple praying. I included this note:

> Dear Don. May the Lord allow us to grow old together—and in His grace—like this dear old couple.

Even as I wrote it, I had an odd clutching within my spirit, as though I knew we'd never achieve that status. But I shook off the premonition, afraid thinking about it would make it come true.

Yes, I had planned for us to grow old together, the way my grandparents did. But that didn't happen, and I have great chunks of memories I can't share with anyone, such as "Who was that couple who lived next door to us in married housing? The ones with the squeaky bed?"

But while I heard the sounds a dying man makes, many of you have heard the sounds a dying *marriage* makes, and my heart goes out to you. Or perhaps you are a "married single" who watches your traditional family neighbors leave for a Saturday afternoon picnic or ski trip, and you think about the circumstances that keep your family from such outings.

We have to be careful, though, not to get dreams and reality confused. After all, plenty of married folks *are* growing old together and envying those of us who aren't married. In fact, as I speak, I often quote Isaiah 54:5—"For your Maker is your husband"—and I've lost track of the number of married women who have hugged me afterward and whispered, "I wish I had *your* husband." So let's not waste energy on longing for the dreams that haven't come true. Instead, let's look for ways to find the joy in today.

Accepting the Future

I learned to see each day's joy years ago. And I learned it from someone who at first glance didn't have anything to offer other than an empty seat in her breakfast booth.

Early that morning, I had peered into the mirror as I brushed back the hair from my face. The wing of gray at my right temple had widened almost overnight. I tossed the brush onto the bathroom counter. It was definitely a day for breakfast at our favorite coffee shop.

The Coffee Shop in the middle of Mount Kisco, New York, was one of those narrow restaurants too busy serving food to bother with the latest tile colors or soda machines. The five booths and dozen counter stools had witnessed almost 40 years of World Series arguments, weather complaints and social changes. Through it all, the grill sizzled with over-easy eggs and plump hamburgers.

The counter stools were always occupied first, so we usually had no trouble getting a booth. That morning, however, even the booths were filled. We three stood by the door for a moment, surrounded by the combined smells of bacon grease, grilled bagels and strong coffee—wondering if anyone was about to leave.

Suddenly, an elderly woman in the back booth waved for us to join her. After our move from Michigan, we'd quickly learned that New Yorkers are used to sharing their space, so it wasn't an unusual invitation.

We smiled our thanks at the woman and walked toward her. Holly slid into the booth next to her, while Jay and I sat across from them. I thanked the woman for her kindness, then introduced myself and both teens.

She smiled and nodded, but merely pointed to her ear and shook her head. *Oh dear, she's deaf,* I said to myself.

We three sat uncomfortably silent, while our hostess continued with her breakfast. Her red, arthritic hands cut the poached egg on toast as I stared at my own hands, fearing—knowing— someday they would look like hers.

Wasn't it enough I'd found the new streak of gray just that morning? Did I need this second reminder of my mortality, too?

As I looked at Jay and Holly and flashed my standard "It's okay" smile, her hands still moved in my side vision. I forced my thoughts to other details of her person. The collar of her flowered navy blue dress peeked over the top of her tightly buttoned maroon sweater. Tinted glasses sat on the end of her nose.

Her hair was silver and covered by a bright blue winter cap. What color had her hair been? Nondescript brunette like mine?

Or chestnut—its red highlights tossing bits of sunlight toward her admiring beau?

Had her swollen hands once gently held babies who had long since grown up and left for exotic places, remembering her only at Christmas and Mother's Day—if then? Had those same hands tenderly sponged the feverish forehead of an ill husband who, despite her care, died, leaving her to grow old alone?

She put her knife and fork across the plate, drank the last of the mug's weak coffee and then leaned toward Holly. "Why do you go to bed at night?" she asked.

Because we had thought she was probably mute as well as deaf, her question momentarily startled us. Finally Holly shrugged and answered, "Because I'm tired?"

The woman leaned forward, the sparkle in her eyes suddenly apparent. "Because the bed won't come to you!"

We three laughed appreciatively then, so she tapped the table surface in front of Jay. "If I put a quarter and a five-cent piece here, and the five-cent piece rolled off, why wouldn't the quarter roll off, too?"

Jay and I looked at each other in puzzlement. The woman smiled as she supplied the answer with obvious delight. "Because the quarter has more sense!"

Her unexpected play on words was so comical that we all laughed. I waited for another riddle, but she busied herself, gathering up her newspaper and purse. Holly stood up to let her out of the booth.

She smiled at me, patted Holly's shoulder, gripped Jay's hand in farewell and was off, her head up and her stooped shoulders straightened—momentarily, at least—against the day.

The booth suddenly seemed empty. My immediate sense of loss was so evident that Holly asked, "What's wrong, Mom?"

I stared at her for a moment. Actually, nothing was wrong, but something was indeed gone. Yes, that was it—her joy. That dear, elderly woman had given us a moment of unexpected joy, a brief time of serendipity, and I wanted to relish it, for at least a little longer.

In those few moments we'd spent with her, I'd seen no self-pity, no laments for what she had lost and no admonishment that I enjoy these "best days of my life" with my children. She had merely invited us to share her private joy—and, in doing so, had shown us a more noble way to face challenges.

I smiled at the memory of her sparkling eyes. And the memory helped me accept the new gray streak in my hair as merely another well-earned milestone. *When I'm her age*, I told myself, *I hope I'm also teaching others to grab today's joy.*

And for now, I'll rejoice in what I have instead of lamenting what I've lost. And that's not a bad lesson to have learned so early in life.

Letting Go

If we've done our job right, our children won't want to stay around us forever. Oh, they'll enjoy coming home at holidays, maybe, but for the most part, they'll go their own way. And that's supposed to be the end result of all of our parenting—to make them so strong that they will be able to take care of themselves.

So what do we do when they're gone—the very ones who have absorbed our every waking moment for so long? We have to start thinking about that chapter in our lives long before it happens.

I've always enjoyed taking side trips. When Jay and Holly were little, they went wherever I took them. By their early teens, they still went but complained a lot. In their midteens, I could get them to go only if I let each of them take a friend along.

Soon we were to the point where they were usually involved in a church activity or sporting event, so if I wanted to go to a particular concert or special program, I went with *my* friends. I was comfortable with that because we had arrived at the new stage in little steps.

I didn't want to be so dependent on my children that I couldn't function once they left the nest. Nor did I want to whine, "Why don't you call me more often?"

Even then, I knew they wouldn't call me as much as I'd wish. But my goal was for my two teens to turn into mature, responsible adults, which would allow me to know I had done my job well. And, yes, all too soon I was wrapping prayers around their little vessels as they sailed off without me.

Cutting the Apron Strings

When Jay graduated from high school, he, Holly and I celebrated at our favorite restaurant.

One present from me was a narrow box containing two strips of blue flowered material. As Jay folded back the tissue, he stared at the vaguely familiar pattern for a long moment. Finally, I said, "That's my most important present of all, Honey. Those are my apron strings to symbolize that you are no longer tied to them."

Jay grinned, and Holly immediately exclaimed, "Great! Next year, do I get apron strings, too?"

Groan. The years were passing far too quickly. But sure enough, just a few days later (it seemed) there we were again at our same favorite restaurant. This time it was Holly who was opening presents for *her* high school graduation. When she got to the narrow box, she smiled and quickly tore off the paper. Inside, indeed, were the strings from my second apron. Attached was this note:

Dear Holly,

As Jay can tell you, I'll often try to take this gift back.
But here are my apron strings to say I really am trying
to let you go. Go forward with God.

Much love,
Mom

Both of those evenings were milestones in our finding new
ways to relate—no longer just as parent and child, but as adult
to adult. In the process of building new relationships with my
children, I've discovered new ways of relating are gifts to be trea-
sured.

And, in case you're wondering, aprons aren't as old fash-
ioned as some folks might think. Even though I don't cook the
way I used to, those aprons covered my work clothes when I got
in late and had to throw together a spaghetti dinner. They also
went around little waists when it was time to make salt and baking soda school projects. For us, cut apron strings symbolized
my letting go. What will work for you when that time comes?
And believe me, that time will come.

Since the presentation of those gifts, I've often thought
about the celestial apron strings our heavenly Father has given
us. He protects us, yes, but He also gives us freedom. Freedom
to choose our daily routine, freedom to invite Him into our
decisions (or not), even freedom to discard His loving guidelines. At times, I wish He had never cut those strings for me,
since I haven't always chosen the right way. But the fact that He
gives us choices should be encouraging, too, since it says we are
not powerless. We *can* choose the right way, including inviting
Him into the daily challenges of single parenting. And that's a
great gift, indeed.

Planning Ahead

In preparation for letting go, I began early to adjust to a schedule that included things I like to do. I actually made a list of the local museums and tourist attractions Jay and Holly hadn't been interested in. But I also knew such touristy activity would get old fast, so I pondered ways to expand my speaking and writing. (Kentucky women have to be kept busy to keep us out of trouble.) Besides, I didn't want to drive my *adult* children nuts—after all, I had concentrated on them for so many years! I'd seen in the lives of my friends the damage clingy mothers can do, so I thought about ways to keep Jay and Holly as my friends long after they stopped being my responsibility.

But most single mothers aren't to this place yet. They're still trying to find lost mittens and dropping the children off at the sitter's. Or they are juggling early teen schedules, worrying about unsupervised activities and trying to plan quality time. If you're one of those moms, "Honey, hang in there! It does get better."

What you're going through now is absolutely exhausting, but your turn *is* coming. You will be able to breathe at a normal rate again.

But even as I typed that last paragraph, I thought of the old saying, "Just when a mother thinks her work is finished, she becomes a grandmother."

So we're in mothering for the long haul, but we have the challenge and joy of watching our loving influence make a difference in another's life. That's heady stuff.

Having Strength for Others

A few weeks ago, I watched the classic film *The Grapes of Wrath*. Perhaps because it was produced during the Great Depression when folks were desperate for hope, it ended on a happier note than the book did. I was struck by the mother's incredible strength as she held her family together. I especially liked her refusal to give up. When the sky is caving in, someone must stand with arms thrust upward saying, "Here, come stand by me. It's going to be okay."

That's the type of woman I want to be.

One thing that can keep us from having such strength, though, is our tendency to listen to the wrong voices.

Whenever I run into anyone who predicts failure for my latest venture, I try to remember the story Kim told about her son, Trey, who was pitching in the Little League championship game. The tie run was on third base; the winning run on second. On the mound, Trey leaned toward home plate, trying to concentrate on the catcher's signals for this last pitch of the game.

Suddenly, the fans of the opposing team began to jeer, calling, "Loser! You'll never get it over the plate!"

Kim clutched her hands together and whispered, "Come on, Trey. Don't listen to the voices. Remember what we talked about this morning."

On their way to the park, Kim had sensed the lad's anxiety and had asked him what was wrong.

"I hate it when the other team's fans yell at me," he answered.

"Do they come onto the field and yell in your face?" she asked, feigning naivete.

"Well, no," he conceded. "But they make me feel bad, and I can't concentrate."

"Don't listen to the voices," his mom said. "Look at your catcher. Think about the next pitch. Their voices can't take away your ability. But they *can* cause you to stop yourself."

Now, on the mound, Trey stared at the batter, went into his windup—and delivered strike three to win the game.

Yes, we single mothers may have folks telling us we're losers. But they have power only if we listen to them. In fact, the voices may come to us from the past—a drunken parent, a cruel classmate, a thoughtless teacher, an unstable coworker.

I know about those voices from the past—they are featured on the mental tapes I'm prone to replay. But I have finally learned to replace those old tapes with new, strengthening ones:

God didn't bring me this far to leave me alone.

I can *do this.*

This, too, shall pass.

And my feisty favorite: *Keep hanging on to the Lord and don't let the "turkeys" win!*

What new messages can you come up with to replace the old ones you've been playing?

Fighting for My Wrinkles

When I look in the mirror today, I see a Titus 2:3-4 woman, someone who has the privilege of encouraging—and teaching—younger women.

Do I miss the smooth, firm skin of my youth? Of course. But do I *grieve* its loss? No, each line represents another milestone in my journey toward becoming the woman God wants me to be.

Recently, I had my annual PR photo taken by a local studio. Since the prints were a simple head and shoulders shot, I expected them back within a day or two. But when I called, the photographer said I couldn't have them for another week; she'd sent them to the finishing department to have the lines around my eyes airbrushed out.

"I don't want those lines brushed out," I said. "I've worked hard for them."

"But," she pointed out unnecessarily, "they make you look middle-aged."

"I *am* middle-aged," I declared. "Leave my wrinkles alone."

I refused to give in, and the photos were ready to be picked up that afternoon. And, clearly, the wrinkles of years past were all there, unretouched and undiminished by cosmetic artifice.

Yes, every feature, every contour, every experience line was intact; each one a joyous witness to the years the Lord and I have walked in fellowship together; each one a precious reminder of life's tears and joys; each one a powerful testimony to the love and devotion invested in my wonderful kiddos, Jay and Holly.

And these same lines are also harbingers of promise—there are exciting adventures and fulfilling experiences awaiting me in the years ahead. And always—I trust—those experiences will continue to transform me into the woman God wants me to be.

Once More with Feeling

- Don't waste energy by envying those couples who are growing old together. Plenty of marrieds are envying us singles.
- Accept the future by looking for the joys promised by each new day.
- Rejoice in what you have instead of lamenting what you've lost.
- Be ready to let go when the time comes. Of course, it's tough to release our children. But if we've done our job right, our children will be strong enough to go on without us.
- Plan ahead for the day when your children will be out of your nest, and you will have time for those things you wanted to do.
- Remind yourself that your hectic schedule *now* will make the coming years easier. So for now, hang in there!

· You were strong for your children when they needed your strength. Even after they are gone and on their own, others will still be there who will need you to be strong for them.

· Accept the honor of being a Titus 2:3-4 woman—someone who has the privilege of teaching and encouraging younger women.

· Wear your wrinkles with pride. They are your badge of honor for all the years you have invested in your family.

CHAPTER THIRTEEN

New Adventures Are Ours to Grab. Let's Be Ready for Them!

"For I know the plans I have for you," declares the LORD, "plans to prosper you and not to harm you, plans to give you hope and a future."

JEREMIAH 29:11

We've all heard the saying, "When life hands you lemons, make lemonade!" One of my favorite stories illustrates that thought.

A church's new minister always left written instructions for his staff. A janitor who could not read or write was fired when he failed to respond to the written messages.

But instead of giving in to discouragement, the man began his own cleaning business and eventually became very wealthy.

One day, his banker was astounded when he discovered his customer's illiteracy. "Just imagine where you'd be if you could read and write!" he exclaimed.

The man smiled. "I'd be a janitor at the corner church."[1]

Know What You Truly Want

When you're faced with a major decision, remember the biblical three-step process: pray, read the Word, and seek godly counsel. But what if you've done all that and you still don't have a clear answer?

When that happens to me, I know I'm probably fighting fear. In those moments, I ask myself, *A year from now, what are you going to wish you had done?*

I've asked myself that twice—when we moved from Michigan to New York and again when we moved to Colorado. And both times, I've been glad that I took a deep breath and grabbed the adventure.

Maintain a Positive Attitude

Remember, in this life, we never get everything we want. For all of us, life is filled with trade-offs; for everything we lose, we gain something else. And for everything we gain, we lose.

That's why it is so important that we know what we truly want. And many times, our attitude decides the final outcome.

Discard Fear

I remember when we were considering the move to Colorado. I was convinced the Lord was offering me an incredible opportunity, and

Jay wanted out of New York. There was only one hang-up: Holly's fears. How could I convince her she *would* survive?

Of course, I was praying constantly. Then one evening while Jay and Holly attended a youth activity, Doug and Lou, friends from church, invited me over for dinner. We chatted about parenting and our jobs, and Doug told about his work with the disabled. One story he told offered the encouragement I needed.

As part of his training, Doug had worked in a hospital. A man had been there for several weeks recovering from an accident, but he was still having trouble walking.

The doctors insisted this patient had no physical reason for the tiny, cautious steps he insisted upon, but he ignored their pronouncements that he could walk normally. Then they assigned Doug to him.

The first afternoon with the man, Doug watched him take those fear-filled steps and then asked why he walked like that.

"I'm afraid I'll fall," the man replied.

I would have told the man, "You won't fall," but Doug merely asked another question: "Did you ever fall when you were a kid."

"Sure, lots of times," the man said.

"Where?"

"On the grass."

Doug nodded and asked, "How about when you were older? Did you ever fall then?"

The man smiled. "Sure. I played softball. I was always falling, diving after a ball or for a base."

Doug nodded again. "Okay, we're going for a walk, and I'm going to trip you. You're going to fall. Then you're going to see it's all right."

The man wasn't sure he could do that, but Doug coached him outside to the hospital lawn. As they walked along, talking about their favorite sports teams, Doug suddenly tripped him—just as he had promised he would—and the man sprawled in the grass.

For a moment, he lay still, as though he was mentally checking for broken bones. Everything was okay. He stood up and grinned at Doug. Then he bounced up and down and even gave a little jump. He was going to be just fine.

That evening when I picked the kiddos up from the youth group, I put my arm around Holly and told the story.

Then I gave her an extra squeeze. "So, Honey, I'm going to trip you," I said. "But you're going to see God is leading us, and it's going to be okay."

She gave me one of her exasperated huffs, but she knew there would be no turning back. Yes, she "plowed ground" with her fingers as she tried to hang on to the familiar during our drive West. But it didn't take her long to settle in, make new friends and decide she really liked it in Colorado.

Whew!

Be Bold

Most of the biblical psalms we find so uplifting were written during times of difficulty, and most of the epistles with their messages of joy and love were sent from prison. How's that for holy boldness?

My teaching buddy, Carl, kept this quotation on his board: "What happens isn't as important as how you react to it."

Yes, our attitude will make the difference in whether we're open to the good things God wants to give us. But often we get just what we expect out of life.

Years ago, I invited a perfectly healthy aunt to have dinner with us the following Thursday.

Her reply was simple: "Oh, I can't plan anything. I might be sick."

She missed numerous opportunities to have fun because she was afraid of taking a risk.

Have Courage

A while back, I heard a minister say, "Courage is fear that has already said its prayers." I like that. When we're afraid, we exaggerate our fears and say, "I'll never make it."

Do you recall the account in Numbers 13 when the spies returned from their survey of the Promised Land?

The fighters, like Caleb, said, "We *can* do it!"(see Num. 13:30).

But the tired ones lied, both to themselves and to the people, and said they couldn't possibly do it. "We seemed like grasshoppers in our own eyes, and we looked the same to them" (v. 33).

That's the way we feel when we're really up against it. Remember that the sin is *not* in being afraid but in what we do with that fear.

Take Risks

I still remember the question my high school senior literature teacher posed to us: "Who's more brave? The person who rushes to save another without thinking or the one who has time to consider it and still goes to the rescue?"

Even these years later, my answer is the same: "The one who knows what he's risking."

At one time or another, like the spies of Numbers 13, we all have Jordan Rivers in our lives—and we're afraid to cross over to the other side. And, because we fear the risk and fail to cross, we are unable to accept what the Lord offers us. When that happens, we end up living small, pointless lives. Yet we really face no risk when we simply obey and go where the Lord leads.

What wonderful things we would experience if we claimed God's promises and started living life boldly.

Keep a Merry Heart

When we lived in New York, we ventured down to watch the Macy's Thanksgiving Day parade with friends—and with countless thousands of others. It was an incredible day of seeing the displays that had long been part of our holiday traditions, but only on TV. The best part of the day for me, though, was meeting a subway elevator operator.

For long hours each day he was trapped in a box under the streets of New York City and breathing air thick with dirt and fumes. I wouldn't have blamed him if he'd been grumpy and complained about being stuck underground. But he greeted us cheerfully and asked where we were from.

When he had delivered us to our requested level, he wished us well, asked us to come back again and added a cheerful, "I luv ya."

Later as we were waiting for the subway train on the lower level, we could hear him singing as he strolled in front of the elevator, waiting for his next batch of passengers. Rather than allowing himself to become embittered or discouraged by his lot in life, he chose to bring freshness and joy to those who shared his day, even for those few moments.

So rather than fretting about our lot in life, let's become like the subway singer and give others reason to smile at our joyful spirit.

Waste No Time on Regrets

Regrets can keep us from accepting a bright new future, too. Years ago, I told Morrie, a Dutch friend, about my worry that I'd sold some furniture for too low a price.

His quick advice has since gotten me through more than mere furniture sales: "You've made your decision. Now live with it."

So even as we pray, we need to make a conscious effort to stop the "if only's": "If only I hadn't moved . . ." or "If only I hadn't taken that job . . ."

A couple of summers ago, a friend was back in her hometown visiting relatives. While her children enjoyed a special outing with the cousins, she drove by the house where she had lived before her divorce. She felt almost as though she should pull into the driveway and honk the horn for her husband to help with the groceries.

But, of course, that was impossible, and she drove on with tears in her eyes. *Why didn't I have the good sense to enjoy those years instead of always looking for perfection?* she wondered.

Relief came only as she prayed, asking the Lord's forgiveness for not having appreciated His many blessings. And then she asked Him to help her see the joy and preciousness of each new day. In that moment, she let go of the past and was willing to move forward.

Stay Thankful

In 1981, Chet Bitterman, Jr., a Wycliffe missionary in Bogota, Columbia, was kidnapped. For a long while, his father furiously paced his Pennsylvania home, wondering how he could rescue his son, when he suddenly heard within his spirit, "Give thanks."

To give thanks was the last thing Chet, Sr., wanted to do. He'd already seriously pondered rounding up an armed group of his friends, flying into the South American city and taking it apart, brick by brick.

The Act of Giving Thanks
But as he struggled with the Spirit's witness in his heart, he realized the command was to *give* thanks, not *feel* thanks. As he wondered what he could possibly be thankful *for*, he remembered his

son had memorized hundreds of Scripture verses.

Surely those verses are encouraging him right now, he thought. And he immediately gave thanks for the reassurance and courage the Word of God was giving Chet, Jr., at that very moment.

The Benefit of Giving Thanks

Upon further reflection, Chet, Sr., added further thankfulness for his son's physical strength and emotional stability. The list grew. When young Chet's body was found in an abandoned bus 48 days later, the spirit of thankfulness that had already been sown helped his father open his heart to the comfort the Lord wanted to give.

Remembering that account has helped me often in this life of singlehood. I decided if Chet, Sr., could find something to give thanks for in the midst of his great emotional pain, surely I could, too. Amazingly, I have done that, many, many times.

The Attitude of Giving Thanks

A thankful attitude allows us to live life with joy and to rejoin life when we feel momentarily estranged from it. More than that, having a thankful spirit helps us laugh and love with genuine abandon. For without thankfulness, we would wither inwardly and be in danger of becoming bitter, mirthless creatures, a drag on ourselves and everyone around us.

So rejoice and give thanks. If you haven't found something today to give thanks for, you haven't looked very hard. If you need some help in that department, consider these three simple suggestions from writer/editor Elizabeth Sherrill that are guaranteed to make every day a day of thanksgiving.

1. Every day, surprise someone with a thank-you.
2. Every day, thank God for something you have never until now thanked Him for.

3. Every day thank God for something about which you are not now happy.[2]

Practice them, yes, even when you don't feel like giving thanks! The ongoing act will in itself grow the spirit of thankfulness and thanksgiving in your heart.

So try it. You'll like it. I know.

Be Open to the Lord's Blessings

Keeping my life open to the Lord's blessings is a lesson I especially needed as a single mother—but one I had to learn the hard way.

The Opportunity

I met Marta Gabre-Tsadick, the first woman senator of Ethiopia, at a Michigan conference grounds. Her very posture announced authority and grace. Stately and beautiful, she was everything I wasn't.

My pastor, who was at the same conference that week, knew of Marta's renown and invited her to tell our church about the Marxist takeover of her beloved Ethiopia—the world's oldest Christian nation.

Impulsively, I asked Marta to stay with my family the weekend she would speak. She accepted, and I assumed the matter was settled.

The Self-Doubt

Several weeks later, however, a friend who had visited Marta's home commented that Marta had served her a glass of water from a tray. Outwardly, I nodded at how much that sounded like the gracious Marta. But inwardly, I cringed.

Serving a glass of water from a tray? I couldn't remember if I owned a tray, let alone if I knew how to serve from it. At our home, if someone comes into the kitchen and asks for a drink of water, I'm apt to continue whatever I'm doing and wave toward the cabinets, saying, "Sure. The glasses are up there. The water's in the refrigerator. Help yourself."

So what in the world was I thinking of when I decided to invite someone like *Marta* into my home?

As the days passed, I became more tense. I considered buying a tray and practicing with it. However, the thought of stumbling and dumping the water into her lap changed my mind.

My self-imposed misery continued. I even thought of calling Marta and saying a family emergency had forced me to withdraw my offer and that we'd provide a motel room instead. No, my statement wouldn't be a lie—my inner turmoil had already resulted in several sleepless nights. And, believe me, if I'm not sleeping, it's a *family* emergency!

The Petition

Finally, I did what I should have done when the trauma first started—I prayed. As I poured out my insecurities, I knew God already knew the details, but I needed to hear myself say what he already knew.

I described the contrast between my background and Marta's and listed all the reasons why I couldn't possibly have such a dignified woman in *my* home. Then I had the good sense to shut up and listen.

The Release

In that next moment, it was just as though the Lord was saying, "Marta is doing a good job at being Marta. Now you must do equally well at being who you are."

The room wasn't suddenly filled with a golden light, and no trumpet blast heralded a message. But a deep calm settled over me and freedom rushed in. We'd had guests before; I'd just haul out my best company recipes and invite my pastor and his wife over, too, to help carry the conversation.

The Fellowship

When the appointed weekend arrived, Marta, her husband, Deme, and their two sons proved to be such delightful guests that I found myself concentrating on the exciting story of their miraculous escape from Ethiopia rather than on myself.

Afterward, Marta offered to help with the dishes, but I insisted she leave them for me. I urged her to rest before speaking that evening.

Reluctantly, she left the kitchen as I cleared the counter. But, in a few minutes, she was back. "May I please have a glass of water?" she asked in her softly accented voice.

Without thinking, I answered, "Sure. The glasses are in the cabinet, and the water's in the refrigerator. Help yourself."

The words were barely out of my mouth when embarrassment swept over me. How could I have spoken like that to Marta, of all people. I know God had reminded me to be myself, but this was going too far. I bit my lip in frustration.

The Blessing

That night, as we prepared to leave for the church, Marta gave me a special hug. Then, with her hand on the doorknob, she suddenly turned back to me. Tears were in her eyes as she said, "Thank you for making us feel so much at home here. For two years we have not felt part of a family until now."

She paused, then shared her great hurt. "We had to leave our families behind—our parents and brothers. Thank you for allowing us to be part of *your* family. Thank you for letting me get my own water."

By then, I was crying, too, but with joy. I had almost allowed my insecurities to rob me of an incredible blessing.

And Move Out in Faith

With the Lord's help—and as we ask Him to bring His good out of our pain—we can do more than merely survive our situation; we can actually be victorious over it.

But we can't get arrogant about our ability to face the challenges ahead—as I learned when we were living in Michigan.

John and Elizabeth Sherrill had invited me to Chappaqua, New York, to talk about a writing project. I was elated—and nervous as a cat.

New York was the end of the world to me then. How could I fly to LaGuardia Airport, rent a car and drive the hour north on those mysterious eastern parkways? But John sent me a map as though he had confidence in my ability to handle such a huge challenge.

The plane landed safely, and I picked up the rental car. I studied my map that, if followed correctly, would lead me through the area around LaGuardia until I could pick up the route to head north.

Pray—a Lot

And I prayed constantly: "Well, Lord, you know I have the worst sense of direction in the world. But I trust You to guide me and get me there safely and back to the airport on time."

With a giant sigh, I put the car into gear and started out through the gate. At each stoplight, I reexamined the map.

Which way, Lord? I prayed.

Amazingly, at every turn I just knew the way to go. At one point, the street sign had been knocked down. I cocked my head to decipher the way it had been pointing, but it was as though He was sitting right at my elbow, saying, "Turn left at the next stop."

It was an amazing day. Not only did I spend the day with the Sherrills, but I also drove through New York City—both miracles for a Harlan County, Kentucky, gal.

Let Him Take It from Here

My plane back home landed at Detroit's Metro Airport right on time. I was 20 minutes from home and would drive a route I'd driven dozens of times. As I located my car in the parking lot, I didn't *say* it, but my attitude was one of "Thanks, God. Now I'll take it from here!"

An hour later, with my frustration growing by the minute, I was still trying to get off Ecorse Road. It wasn't until I prayed again to ask for help that I finally got onto I-94 and headed home.

Since then I've often found myself praying, "Don't let me take it from here again. *Your* will only."

I learned that night I can't always handle the most familiar things, so I have to trust the unfamiliar to Him, too. But I've also learned He wants to help us get back on the right road—if we'll let Him.

Ask, Seek, Knock

Because I am God's child, He is concerned about every aspect of my life. I like those three verbs in Luke 11:9: "*Ask* and it will be given to you; *seek* and you will find; *knock* and the door will be opened to you" (emphasis added).

"Ask," "seek" and "knock" are words of action for us. Even as much as we long to be rescued from problems, we still are responsible for the results. The Lord has promised to help us, to direct us, but we still have to take that first step in faith.

He's standing by us, waiting for us to ask Him to help us juggle all our scary responsibilities. And as we do, we will find that wonderful experiences *are* ahead for us—if we'll just allow the Lord to give them to us.

Glory in the Darkness

We three had been in Colorado only a few weeks when I dropped Jay off at high school at 4 A.M. to catch the bus for a regional event. I had a lot on my mind, including the roof damage from the latest hail storm, the new short circuit in the car's engine, wild critters trying to move into the attic—well, you get the picture.

That morning, instead of going home, I drove to a nearby park noted for its majestic red rock formations. I needed to connect with God—and I thought I could do that best in His world instead of in mine.

As I entered the blackness of the park, I pulled off the narrow road and got out to study the heavens, hoping the beauty of the star-filled sky would offer some encouragement. Suddenly, a bright green meteor shot across the full length of the sky. Stunned, I said aloud, "Oh! Thank You!" as I watched the trail. As the vivid color faded into the horizon, my problems didn't seem as heavy as before. Oh, they were far from being solved, and I still had to deal with the new problems on top of the ones I was already carrying—but I knew that scene would remain with me in the days ahead.

I also knew I would never have seen the Creator's glory except in the darkness. And that's how it is with the challenges we face as single parents. We have the opportunity to be more in tune with His help and His very presence because of our situation. Often, all we have to do is look *up*. Remember, Daniel of the Old Testament was not saved *from* the lion's den—he was saved *in* it.

Three at the Altar

I started this book with the assurance that both of my children turned out to be wonderful adults despite having been raised in a single-parent household. But even after we had survived cross-country moves, financial crises and life's various challenges, we still had a surprise or two waiting—especially when Holly got engaged.

As she and I were making her wedding plans, I realized she seemed increasingly melancholy. Then, one evening, she lamented that her dad wasn't there to walk her down the aisle. We both cried a little, but she wiped her eyes and decided to ask Jay to escort her. I started praying right then that his usual tendency to shy away from the spotlight wouldn't keep him from acceding to her wishes.

The next evening, the three of us gathered in the living room, and Holly made her request. In anticipation of this moment, Jay had prepared a little speech. He got only as far as "Holly, that's Dad's job . . ." before she—in typical Aldrich family style—stopped him from finishing his sentence.

"But Dad's dead!" she wailed.

"Believe me, Holly, I know," he sighed. "What I was going to say is that's Dad's role, but *Mom* has been the one who's held this family together. *She* should walk you down the aisle."

Now it was my turn to wail. "But Jay, I want to be the mother of the bride," I protested, ignoring the enormous compliment he had just given me. "I want to stand up and turn to watch Holly come down the aisle."

Poor Jay. Now he had two crying women to calm down. While he patted first one, then the other on the shoulder, Holly and I blew our noses. Then we all settled down to discuss possible solutions. After my usual open-ended prayer of "Lord, please help," we finally decided we would "tag team" the event: Jay would walk

Holly down the aisle to my pew; then I would step out and give the declaration in answer to the pastor's question "Who escorts this woman to this man?" (Notice we don't give away women in *this* family.)

No, the solution wasn't our first choice—that one had included her dad—but it was a good one. In fact, as it turned out, the three of us standing together before the altar provided a touching visible symbol of the team we had been. And all because we had invited the Lord into the problem, analyzed our choices and adjusted to the solution. Not a bad strategy for handling any single-parenting situation.

Now, I realize many of you wish you could apply this solution to your daughter's future marriage. Instead, you will face the challenge of the presence of your ex-husband's new wife and family. But I know you can handle the situation with grace and perhaps even humor. After all, I've seen several of my friends do exactly that. For the sake of family peace—and sincere smiles for the wedding photos—they set aside painful memories and bit back sharp comments. And you know what? They tell me they slept better after the ceremony because of their decision to enjoy the day. Good for them.

So face challenges with your head high, dear single mother. You have great strength—and a bright future.

Once More with Feeling

- · When life hands you lemons, make lemonade.
- · Know what you truly want out of life, because none of us gets everything we want. That's why life is full of trade-offs.
- · When you're faced with a major decision, remember the biblical three-step process: pray, read the Word, seek godly counsel.

- When you're fighting fear, ask yourself, *A year from now, what will I wish I had done?*
- When you make a decision, your attitude often decides the final outcome. So maintain a positive attitude toward life.
- Put aside your fears and, with boldness and courage, be ready to take some risks.
- What happens isn't as important as how you react to it.
- Keep a merry heart and give others reason to smile at the memory of your joyful spirit.
- Waste no time on regrets. Instead, let go of the past, and ask God to help you see the joy and preciousness of each new day.
- Always give thanks, even when you don't feel thankful. The act renews a spirit of thankfulness within.
- Don't allow your insecurities to rob you of the incredible blessings God has in store for you.
- With the Lord's help—and as you ask Him to bring His good out of your pain—you can do more than merely survive your situation; you can actually be victorious over it.
- Remember, in Christ, you are God's child, and He is concerned about every aspect of your life. He has promised to help you, so ask, seek and knock in faith.
- Like Daniel, you aren't protected *from* bad situations— but through God's grace, you are saved *in* them.

Notes

1. A. Philip Parham, *Letting God: Christian Meditations for Recovering Persons* (New York: HarperCollins Publishers, 1987), reading for March 30.
2. Elizabeth Sherrill, *Journey into Rest* (Minneapolis, MN: Bethany House, 1990), pp. 158-160.

Inspiring Reading for Women

Women: God's Secret Weapon
God's Inspiring Message to Women of Power, Purpose and Destiny
Ed Silvoso
ISBN 08307.28872

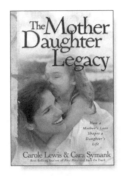

The Mother-Daughter Legacy
How a Mother's Love Shapes a Daughter's Life
Carole Lewis and *Cara Symank*
ISBN 08307.33353

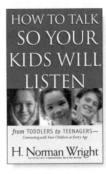

How to Talk So Your Kids Will Listen
From Toddlers to Teenagers—Connecting with Your Children at Every Age
H. Norman Wright
ISBN 08307.33280

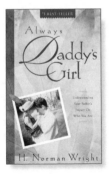

Always Daddy's Girl
Understanding Your Father's Impact on Who You Are
H. Norman Wright
ISBN 08307.27620

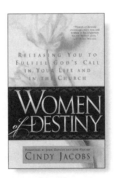

Women of Destiny
Releasing You to Fulfill God's Call in Your Life and in the Church
Cindy Jacobs
ISBN 08307.18648

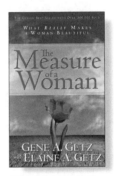

The Measure of a Woman
What Makes a Woman Beautiful
Gene and Elaine Getz
ISBN 08307.32861